Everywhere Home:
A Life in Essays

Fenton Johnson

Sarabande Books
Louisville, KY | Brooklyn, NY

Also by Fenton Johnson

Crossing the River
Scissors, Paper, Rock
Geography of the Heart: A Memoir
Keeping Faith: A Skeptic's Journey among Christian and Buddhist Monks
The Man Who Loved Birds

Documentary narrations:

Stranger with a Camera
La Ofrenda: Days of the Dead
I Just Wanted to Be Somebody

for those who gave and give their lives for others

among them Laurie Johnson Boone (1949-2012)

Library of Congress Cataloging-in-Publication Data

Names: Johnson, Fenton, author.
Title: Everywhere home : a life in essays / Fenton Johnson.
Description: First edition. | Louisville, KY : Sarabande Books, 2017.
Identifiers: LCCN 2016059114 | ISBN 9781941411438 (paperback)
Subjects: LCSH: Johnson, Fenton--Homes and haunts. | Authors, American--21st
century--Biography. | College teachers--United States--Biography. | Gay
men--United States--Biography. | BISAC: BIOGRAPHY & AUTOBIOGRAPHY /
Literary. | LITERARY COLLECTIONS / Essays. | LITERARY COLLECTIONS /
American / General.
Classification: LCC PS3560.O3766 Z74 2017 | DDC 818/.5403 [B] --dc23
LC record available at https://lccn.loc.gov/2016059114

Interior and exterior design by Sarabande Books.

Printed in Canada.
This book is printed on acid-free paper.

Sarabande Books is a nonprofit literary organization.

This project is supported in part by an award from the National Endowment for the Arts. The Kentucky Arts
Council, the state arts agency, supports Sarabande Books with state tax dollars and federal funding from the
National Endowment for the Arts.

Prologue: On Fire

Part 1

Part II

Part III

Part IV

Epilogue: Light in August

Like those wandering monks
who, calling nowhere home, are everywhere home.

—Jane Hirshfield, "To Speech"

Prologue

On Fire
(2016)

I ordered my first drink at the Club 68 in Lebanon, Kentucky, thirty winding country miles east of my childhood home. The Club was owned by Lebanese Christians—a long story, but the short version is that prosperous Anglos have always farmed out what they call vice to black people and rural people and newly arrived immigrants, people the Anglos can trash and persecute and imprison after they service the Anglo obsession with sin. The Irish, the Jews, the dark-skinned people, the hillbillies, and of course the queers, selling hooch or pot or heroin or meth or sex to the prosperous and, for our trouble, thrown in the slammer after the goods are passed but before the money changes hands.

Fleeing violence abroad, these Lebanese Christians settled in Lebanon, a town of five thousand which, some two centuries earlier, Presbyterian Scots had named after the Middle Eastern homeland of the Club 68's owners. An exile and an outlier, Hyleme George, patriarch of the family, situated his nightclubs on the chitlin circuit, an assemblage of roadhouses scattered throughout the then-segregated South, where African American musicians, en route from winters in New Orleans to summers in Chicago, performed in exchange for a room and a meal and a percentage of the door. Fresh from the multicultural patchwork of the Middle East, unburdened by the South's crushing obsession with race, George understood that white audiences would pay to see and hear black artists. He hired a black manager and cross-programmed acts among his clubs, one all-black, another all-white, the third mixed, and the list of the musicians he hired to play in this town is a roll call of midcentury American blues and jazz and rock 'n' roll: B. B. King, Otis Redding, Jimi Hendrix en route from military service at Fort Campbell in western Kentucky to the formation of his own band in Cincinnati, Little Richard, Bo Diddley, Jackie Wilson, the Supremes, James Brown, Ray Charles, Fats Domino, Chuck Berry, Etta James, Sam & Dave, Wilson Pickett, Percy Sledge, Eddie Floyd, Hank Ballard and the Midnighters, Junior Parker, Joe Tex, LaVern Baker, the Coasters, the Shirelles, the Platters, Count Basie, Nat King Cole—not to mention a few white boys tagging along for the ride, among them Creedence Clearwater Revival, the Tommy Dorsey Orchestra, and Steppenwolf.

I had a friend who was sixteen and thus possessed of a driver's license and his parents' car. I had no idea who was playing that night of my first purchased drink and didn't much care. My friend and I were only looking to get drunk and, as was widely known, the clubs in Lebanon served alcohol to anyone tall enough to push a bill across the bar. The Club legally held maybe three hundred people; that night there were easily five hundred, under a ceiling twenty feet high. Most of us were male. All of us were white. This was 1968, at the Club 68, on US Highway 68. I was fifteen years old. Onstage, Ike and Tina Turner and the Ikettes.

I do not recall what Ike and Tina sang. What I recall is the discovery of desire. What Tina Turner did with her body I hadn't conceived that anybody could *do* with a body. As a gay boy unaware that there were words to name what I was, I wasn't in heat in the manner of most men around me. Nonetheless Miss Turner taught me that evening that the body was something more than a suitcase for transporting the brain. Almost fifty years later I of the too-vivid imagination have to work to imagine how she could strut and entice and seduce five hundred screaming drunk Anglo country boys. That is what we call art and she a true artist, though as I write that sentence I speculate that she must have reveled in asserting her power, her black woman artist's power, in one of the few ways and places available to her.

And so I encountered in art, *her* art, the catalyst for my lifelong project of dismantling Western civilization's separation of body from mind, heart from soul, in what was *shown*, not *told* that evening at the Club 68 by Anna Mae Bullock, former Nutbush, Tennessee, Baptist church choir girl: no duality, no separation, love your neighbor as yourself, we are all one in Christ Jesus, we are all one in desire.

Driving home, my drunk friend got us lost and didn't get me to my parents' house until four A.M. For the first and last time, my mother was waiting up. In her expression I understood that she had thought that *I*, her youngest son, was not going to be a hell-raiser like her three previous sons, and she was sorely disappointed. Soon thereafter segregation ended, at least officially, and doors opened for black artists to perform in first-class venues, even in the South. The chitlin circuit faded into history. A few years after that, Tina left Ike. I doubt she ever again performed in a venue so humble. But she had awakened a force that was not to be denied, and though I am not condoning that drunk drive home and though I mourn all those fine men and women lost to AIDS I have no regrets about my forays into the demimonde, the days and nights given over to seeking connection, communion with the gods, with God.

Not long afterward I graduated from high school and went wandering, an ancient and exacting and honorable calling.

*

Later in these pages I will confess that I do not believe in time, that I do not believe in death. Looking out the window on a chill December day in my beloved Kentucky, my left ankle broken and in a cast from an accident involving a hibernating groundhog's hole in the woods surrounding the hermitage of the Trappist monk, mystic, and writer Thomas Merton, I find the sources of that observation so obvious as to need no explanation. The bare trees' raised limbs etch lines against the pale blue winter sky; another six months and these same trees will present a curtain of green. Only the smallest liberation of consciousness is required to understand me, the groundhog, the trees, and you as seamlessly unified and continuous elements of that same cycle of birth and death and rebirth.

"Nothing is absolute. Everything changes, everything moves, everything revolves, everything flies and goes away." That's Frida Kahlo, who knew whereof she spoke. "Pain, pleasure, and death are no more than a process for existence. The revolutionary struggle in this process is a doorway open to intelligence"—*our* intelligence, yours and mine. "The smallest sprout," Walt Whitman writes, "proves that there is no death." Eternal life, a process some call desire and some call God and some have the wisdom to respect in silence.

From *The Sayings of the Desert Fathers*, translated by Sister Benedicta Ward:

> Abba Lot went to see Abba Joseph and said to him, 'Abba, as far as I can I say my little office, I fast a little, I pray and meditate, I live in peace, and, as far as I can, I purify my thoughts. What else can I do?' Then the old man stood up and stretched his hands toward heaven. His fingers became like ten lamps of fire and he said to him, 'If you will, you can become all flame.'

In fiction and nonfiction, my lifelong subject has been the reintegration of desire and the sacred—a lifelong becoming of the flame.

Part I

North of the South, West of the West
(1990)

I grew up in the Kentucky Knobs, a westward-flung, north-west-curling finger of the Appalachians: steep, Catholic-ridden ridges that form a ragged barrier between the ruling-class Presbyterians and gentlemen-farmer Episcopalians of the rolling Bluegrass to the north and east, and the foot-washing Baptists and dirt-poor Pentecostals of the lumpy Pennyrile to the south and west. Across nearly two centuries, the Catholics of the Knobs made our livings from servicing sin, our own and our neighbors'. In spring and summer, when creeks ran full and clear in their limestone beds, distilleries ran round the clock. Men farmed tobacco during the day, worked the night shift making Heaven Hill, Jim Beam, Antique, Maker's Mark. Women raised kids in daylight, worked the bottling plants at night. In fall, the creeks ran low, the distilleries shut down, and we turned to the tobacco harvest.

When your living is tied to sin, you tend toward a liberal view on the subject, a fact our Protestant neighbors appreciated. Over the years, the taverns of my town became ecumenical melting pots, places to practice vice, where, according to my father, you could tell a man's religion by his weapon, or lack of one. Catholics carried guns, Baptists carried knives, Presbyterians stayed in their cars and used the drive-up window, invented, at my family's tavern, to service the demands of their propriety.

The rugged hills kept civilization and the law at bay until the late 1950s, when the town hired its first policeman and its families bought their first televisions. With everyone (literally) watching, television brought California to the Knobs, and with it the sixties, the first decade to reach us more or less on schedule.

My family owned a black-and-white hand-me-down in a fake woodgrain case. On clear nights, the signal was lost to the universe, but on overcast nights it bounced off the clouds into our wide valley. On those nights we picked up fuzzy versions of NBC and CBS, but this was enough: NBC carried Walt Disney, and even in this two-hundred-year-old town of eight hundred people, buried in the Knobs, he had his impact. It would be a cloudy Sunday evening, and the fields that stretched along the east side of the Jackson Highway would be swarming with kids playing fox and hounds and kick the can, and then it would be 7:30 and we would disappear all at once, to our houses or to the houses of neighbors rich enough to own televisions, to watch *Walt Disney's Wonderful World of Color* in black and white.

Courtesy of the *Wonderful World of Color* I came to think of television as synonymous with California. Walter Cronkite broadcast from New York, but the gray walls of his newsroom might be anywhere; there was no mistaking the whereabouts of Disneyland. I saw the streets of endless suburbia, lined with orange trees and washed eternally with sunshine. I saw images of a bucolic countryside where city boys speaking high English led adventurous lives with heroic pets, where smart city folks brought enlightenment and progress to ignorant farmers.

And more: I watched *The Beverly Hillbillies* and *Green Acres* and saw myself, or at least how television presented me to the world. I watched and then went outside, to see the Knobs in a new light: swarming with mosquitoes and smartweed, peopled with yokels, demanding everlasting labor to produce, not oranges and melons and the glamor of Hollywood, but demon booze and tobacco, that evil weed. I watched and compared and, through television, came to know both shame and envy.

California! I dreamed of it on my school bus, kids packed three to a seat and in the aisles. The route wound through hills populated

by white people whose surnames relegated them from birth to peel-
ing clapboard shacks with tin roofs. The kids from these hollers
had no running water and around January the bus got rank; across
February and March I cultivated the habit of taking a deep breath
before climbing aboard. Once we arrived in the county seat, black
children were crammed into an already crowded bus, adding racial tension to the overburdened air. When I could I grabbed a
window seat and looked out, dreaming of a place where there was
no racism, no poverty, hot water for all and no sweat after a day's
work; dreaming of, in a word, California.

*

One spring day in my senior year of high school, I came home
to find my father at the table surrounded by his friends, a fifth of
bourbon open, its cap in the trash. His employer, Seagram, had
awarded me a scholarship, paying all expenses at any college in the
United States. For the first time ever my father offered me a drink,
and I knew, thanks to the company, that I was a man.

And I knew where I was going. Someone asked, and I knew the
answer. I was California-bound, to see in living color the world I
had known in black-and-white, heading for a place as far from and
as different from the family and the old country as any American
place could be.

My father's friends and the parish priest warned him against
letting me go. "He'll come back a hippie," they said, taking care
that I was in earshot. My father knew nothing of California but
what we had seen on television, and that must have worried him,
but he was a man of honor, who believed that I had earned this
choice. He did not stand in my way.

I left three months early, going in June to participate in a national debate tournament, held coincidentally at Stanford, the university I was to attend that fall. The day before I left, a high-school
girlfriend took me out for a drive and to drink beer, and after one
or two cans of Falls City she said, "Watch out for the soup." "The
soup?" I asked. "They put drugs in your soup," she said. "I saw it

on Walter Cronkite," and probably she had. I didn't order soup, my first day in San Francisco, but this was because I was waiting for someone to offer me marijuana, which I had decided to accept. On my second day out, a blonde debater from Beverly Hills sidled up to me and said, "You want to get stoned?" and I knew that yes, I had arrived. I was in California.

Speaking on labor relations, I lost out in the tournament's first round, the judge noting for my benefit that "steel" was pronounced with one syllable, "oil" with two. The speed of my defeat presaged the coming school year, when I returned to Stanford to have my country accent and ways mocked, much to my surprise and disillusionment. After all, I told myself, as children these Californians and I had participated in the same mass culture: the same *CBS Evening News*, the same *Wonderful World of Color*. I had looked forward to counting myself as one of them—I rebelled, grew my hair, burned my bridges—only to find that they did not share my sense of our fellowship. Instead they saw me as I was, a Southern country boy, no matter how long my hair, no matter how much I protested to the contrary. "But I'm not from the South; I'm from Kentucky!" I'd say. "My great-grandfather was a Union soldier! We went with the North!"

"North of what?" someone asked. We were sitting on the floor of the hallway of my freshman dorm; I had been relating some childhood memory to my dorm mates. Their first response had been disbelief, so impossible was it for them to imagine a world so far removed from prosperous suburbia. But I knew how to tell a good story, and I had kept my audience engaged until a listener piped up, "Would you *please* get to the point!" "The point?" I asked, genuinely puzzled. Even then I understood that the telling of the story *was* the point, that the facts mattered less than sharing the communion of the word, the telling and the listening as entry point to a world outside of time. Only now, decades later, can I hear how exotic I must have sounded to these Californians.

When I think about it, which is too often, I compare this small green apple and this large navel orange, Kentucky and California. I compare their virtues: Kentucky, with its pastoral countryside and its abiding sense of belonging and of place, and California, overwhelming in its grandeur and vastness and beguiling acceptance of our limitless ways of being. I count myself lucky to come to an understanding, if a little late, of how worthy each is of being called home, and how important it is to take on the responsibility of defining and preserving the values that make it so. As a man and a writer, it is my dilemma and my good fortune to know both places, living out a quandary as old as this pilgrim nation: neither Kentuckian nor Californian, here nor there, fox nor hound, divided east from west and always somewhere in between.

Catholic in the South
(1990)

"Catholics and muskrats," my father once said, "are never found far from water." Throughout Catholic grade school, my classmates and I received maps, distributed by the Louisville archdiocese, illustrating my father's premise. Entitled "No-Priest Land, USA," the maps colored in black those American counties lacking a Catholic priest. The South was, of course, a sea of black, penetrated by peninsular strips of white, where, true to my father's observation—Catholics had settled along the rivers.

The maps of No-Priest Land didn't identify specific towns or parishes, but it was easy to find my hometown: New Haven, Kentucky, eight hundred solidly Catholic souls. We were a headland in white, surrounded on three sides by dark Protestant hordes. Right on the county line, we were separated from No-Priest Land by the Rolling Fork River—the width, in summer, of a basketball court.

Thirty years later the New South has made inroads into this particular frontier of No-Priest Land, but the contrast can still catch the eye of the observant traveler along the old Jackson Highway, US 31E. North of the Rolling Fork, the countryside is sprinkled with convents and monasteries, among them the Trappist Abbey of Gethsemani, made famous in the writings of Thomas Merton, and the Motherhouse of the activist Sisters of Loretto. Catholic homes in New Haven display the range of papist paraphernalia, inside and out: crucifixes; holy water crucibles; blessed palm hung to protect the house from fire, earthquake, tornadoes, disease; statues of the Virgin protected from the elements by upright bathtubs half-buried in the earth and painted blue. I think of two nineteenth-century wood mosaics of the Sacred Hearts of Mary and Jesus, hanging in my family's home—dark walnut hearts pierced with seven swords of blond maple (Mary) or crowned with golden chestnut thorns (Jesus), both dripping rich cherry blood.

This is civilized voodoo, with no analogue in the spare Protestant homes a few miles to the south. Decorated with Norman Rockwell reproductions and sometimes a plain wooden cross, these living rooms belie little of the darker side of faith, or life.

The question that puzzled me as a child, that puzzles me now when I go back, is what these symbols signify—the differences in states of mind, heart, and soul they imply, between the Catholics of the South and our Protestant neighbors. What follows is a mixture of anecdote and outright conjecture, born of a contrast that years later sticks in my mind, demanding explanation where perhaps none is to be had: the people among whom I grew up kneel to chant Latin with a golden-robed priest as clouds of incense rise to the God of the Old World, enshrined in a gleaming brass monstrance on a marble altar; while across the Rolling Fork, a mile, maybe, to the south, the people I came to know as a teenager gather under tents before a black-suited preacher, to thump and shout and clap their hands for a distinctly New World Jesus.

*

Located at a religious crossroads, the Middle East of the upper South, St. Catherine's Parish took its role seriously. Where children in urban parishes collected pennies to ransom the pagan babies of Korea, we at St. Catherine's collected scraps of aluminum foil to redeem the pagan babies of the cartographically dark counties of Tennessee, Alabama, Georgia, Mississippi, Kentucky itself. Girls favored collecting chewing gum wrappers; not only were they free, they provided a theologically correct excuse for what was otherwise plainly a vice. Cleverly folded one into another, these bits of foil created a kind of origami testimonial to Catholic evangelism—a chain that lengthened through the year. Sometime in May, the Virgin's month, the chain was weighed and sent off to a destination that took such things in exchange, we assumed, for cash, though we never saw the check. For all we knew, the foil was bartered in some dark Atlanta alley for the heathen children themselves.

We did see Protestants, mostly Baptists, in New Haven. Their own counties were dry—they had outlawed the sale of alcohol—and they kept us Catholics in the business of quenching their thirsts. Otherwise, the two religions barely acknowledged each other. Our Nelson County oriented itself to the north, to Louisville and the Catholic counties strung, with the muskrats, along the Ohio River. Across the Rolling Fork, LaRue County looked toward its theological kin farther to the south. No physical barrier existed, of course; there was only the force of social custom. We knew our place, the Protestants knew theirs. "The red fox has his territory, the gray fox has his territory, and they don't mix," my father said. We were the reds, they were the grays. Nobody crossed the line for very long.

Nobody, that is, except my mother. Seventh of eleven children, born on the Protestant side of the Rolling Fork, she grew up wild, partly because her own mother died early. She rode motorcycles, smoked cigarettes, flirted (dangerously, as it turned out) with the Catholics across the river, among whom the more daring Protestants ventured in search of trouble. She met my father in a roadhouse dance hall, where he was recovering, so he said, from a tragic affair with a woman whose glass eye he could not abide. Within months, my mother was baptized, said her first confession, received her first Communion, and spoke her marriage vows, in a six A.M. ceremony attended by no one from either family.

From the perspective of the secularized 1990s it's hard to appreciate the magnitude of my mother's leap from Bible Belt Protestantism into the ritualized pomp of the pre–Vatican II Catholic Church. To help draw the picture, an older sister, an avid collector

of Catholic paraphernalia, supplied a copy of *My Catholic Faith*,
our eighth-grade catechism, underscoring passages the nuns read
aloud with pointed glances at my brothers and sisters and me:

> The Church strongly disapproves of *mixed* marriages.
> From its long experience, the Church knows that mixed
> marriages are rarely happy . . . the non-Catholic part-
> ner is liable to divorce and contract another marriage,
> whereas the Catholic is bound not to take a second
> partner. The proper training of the children becomes
> difficult . . . it is likely that [they will] lose the Faith.

On this last score they were right: of the eight children in my family, six of us have more or less left the Catholic Church, though not for
lack of effort on the part of my devout mother. Incidentally, *My Catholic Faith* also sheds light on the scheduling of the six A.M. wedding:

> The Church shows its *disapproval* of mixed marriages
> even after dispensation has been granted. Sacred func-
> tions, such as the Nuptial Mass and Blessing, are for-
> bidden: the banns are not published. . . . The ceremony
> is not to take place in the church, but in the rectory or
> some other convenient place.

Such as, perhaps, the woodshed; or so our nuns implied.*
Like all the Catholics among whom I lived, I grew up knowing
both that I lived on the edge of a sea of Protestants and that I
knew almost nothing about them. Thirty years after my mother's
conversion, relations between her and her family were strained.
We visited our non-Catholic relatives rarely, never entering their
churches. When my Protestant grandfather died, we had to obtain

---

* Not that the Catholics had a monopoly on propaganda. In later years, Protestant friends told me of films they saw in summer Bible camp that portrayed the
same mixed marriage from the other side: the wife sprawled in bed, still in her
nightclothes, while the husband says carelessly, "We'll have room for that one, but
I don't know what we'll do with the next."

permission from our parish priest to set foot in the church where his funeral was held.

In 1968 all this changed, and suddenly: partly because of rising Catholic tuition, partly because my family's thirty years' war with St. Catherine's clergy reached its Waterloo, my parents removed their last three children from Catholic schools to send us instead to the public high school in my mother's native Protestant county. Each morning we walked the half mile through town, past the curious eyes of our grade school friends (now bound for the parish high school), down to the Boatyard Bridge, where we crossed the Rolling Fork to board the school bus for a circuitous ride to Protestant Hodgenville.

I was fourteen. Incredibly enough, until shortly before, I had believed most of what the nuns taught: virgin births, indulgences, communion hosts that fell from the tongues of careless schoolchildren to burn holes in the church floor. Rock 'n' roll, Vietnam, race riots in nearby Louisville—repercussions from these were reaching my hometown as I entered my teens. Inheritor of my mother's rebellious blood, possessed by the inflexible logic of adolescence, I rejected the Church with the fervor I'd once reserved for my faith.

I considered atheism, but this was too far beyond the pale even for my passionate sensibilities; besides, the sisters had done their work well—I was, and am, a believer, if not in the Catholic Church, at least in *something*. I resolved instead to shop the religion market, in all its Christian diversity. Shortly after crossing the river, I designed for myself an ecclesiastical survey course consisting of Sunday visits to the Protestant churches of each of my high school classmates.

I remember vividly the plainness of those religions, compared to St. Catherine's gaudy mysticism. Statues, monstrances, marble inlaid with gold leaf, stained glass—St. Catherine's had all these to excess. Its interior walls were covered with frescoes painted by Italians imported for the job: angels trailing banners (*Gloria in excelsis Deo*), whole walls covered with patterns of interlocking acronyms (*BVM, IHS*), crucifixes festooned with lilies, pelicans tearing open their breasts to feed their blood to their young. Entering the stark wood-and-plaster whiteness of the Hodgenville Baptist Church, I grasped in a dim way how different the act of seeing itself must be for those who came to their faith in a church so empty of things to look at.

At those Sunday services across the river, I contrasted for the first time these two ways of being in the world. As Catholics we were raised with the notion of man as both inherently fallen and inherently capable of salvation. With the help of God's grace, everyone was a potential candidate for the pearly gates. The Protestant concept of an "elect"—persons designated as saved in advance of life—was foreign, as was the concept that once born again in Christ, salvation was assured, however you might backslide. At St. Catherine's, I had been taught that salvation was an elusive prize. You might be a paragon of virtue, yet in your dying breath curse the hit-and-run driver who laid you low, and so plunge straight to hell, snatching defeat from the jaws of victory. Alternatively, you might live a lifetime of depravation, yet manage that single act of perfect contrition as the car sped away, and so rise to join the angels.

De facto, this understanding made for an appreciation of the precarious nature of life. To my mind, it accounts for the Catholic traditions both of piety and hedonism, since both reflect an intense involvement with the moment at hand. Together with the notorious assertion that we were "the one, true Church," complete with the uppercase C, it accounts as well for our feeling of moral superiority over our Protestant neighbors. *We* had to work for salvation daily, negotiating moment by moment the dark recesses of the soul. Theirs was the easy route, accomplished in broad daylight in front of an emotional crowd and a passionate preacher.

For their part, the Protestants sat comfortable in the knowledge of their majority and in the sense that the land belonged to them and they to it. I recall the patriotism that permeated the Protestant services I attended. The ascendancy of the Kennedys notwithstanding, as Catholics we maintained an uneasy relationship with government, which we understood as tolerating our presence while not exactly welcoming it. As my Protestant friends were quick to point out, our loyalties were divided between Washington and Rome, that quintessence of all that was Old World, decadent, foreign. To enter the Southern Baptist church and find an American flag as the pulpit's most prominent and colorful adornment was to understand that here was an amiable ally of "the God of our forefathers," however those forefathers might bear no relation to *me*.

As an American, schooled in political principles rooted in Protestantism, I was attracted by this easy alliance between democracy and theology. Protestant congregations elected and rejected their preachers. Services were sometimes led by deacons—mere mortals, my classmates' fathers, who had been sanctified by no order other than the votes of their fellow worshipers. The preacher characterized man's relationship with God as downright personal, incorporating a respect for the process of questioning that had no equivalent among Catholics, to whom the inquiring mind was evidence of the devil's presence. I was pleased by the Protestant notion that the route to God was a path open to individual reflection and modification, rather than a collective turnpike whose curves and milestones were dictated from Rome.

All this seemed so rational, so sensible, so *American*, demanding nothing like Catholicism's rigid adherence to orthodoxy. How impressively different from the byzantine theology of my own church—*the* Church. I was sure, for a while, that I'd found that for which I searched: religion based on logic and intellectual consistency.

And yet I left these Protestant services dissatisfied. I had been raised to believe that religion served as humanity's institutional acknowledgment of mystery; in these Protestant churches I found little that was mysterious. These churches bore the imprint of the hands of remembered generations, whereas the Church of my childhood had been shaped by hands outside of time. It was the shaping by those hands—the Catholic Church would call them, collectively, the hand of God—that my Catholic mind found to be the sine qua non, that characteristic which made the Protestantism of the South seem uncomfortably like social exercise.

To attend Easter Midnight Mass as a child was to experience
mystery rendered palpable, the theater of faith. We approached
the church, guided by the light of a few votive candles illuminating
the stained glass windows from within. Inside, in near-pitch darkness, we groped our way up the aisle to sit beneath statues shroud-
ed in mourning robes of purple satin. The service began on the
church steps with the blessing of oil and fire; that same fire spread
through the congregation via hundreds of beeswax tapers passed
from priest to communicant, accompanied by Latin at once foreign
and as familiar as our native tongue: *lumen Christi, flectamus genua, lae-
tare*—these phrases speak to me across time, arousing now as then a
keen sense of the infinite mystery of the word and the world.

Then the litanies, whose interminable, repetitious chantings I
now understand as a kind of meditation: First the Litany of the
Saints, the unabridged version, honoring hundreds of saints (Santa Lucia, *Ora pro nobis*, All you holy virgins and widows, *Misere re
nobis*). Then the Litany of the Blessed Virgin Mary (House of gold,
Ora pro nobis, Mystical rose, *Ora pro nobis*) that recalls the Virgin cults
of the Middle Ages and before, to the goddess worship of ancient
cultures.

And then the dramatic climax: long after midnight, the pipe or-
gan, silent since Holy Thursday, pulls out all stops for the Gloria.
The church lights come up, the priest sheds his white alb and black
stole for shimmering gold, incense rises in clouds, with the tug of a
thread mourning cloths drop from statues, banks of flowers and lit
candelabras appear on the altars, and over all the tower bells reck-
lessly peal, unceasing, their deep-throated voices palely echoed in
the high-pitched clamor of the altar chimes.

For a small child, at once half-asleep and charged with the thrill
of staying up far later than any other night, this was powerful stuff.
I think of the Easter sunrise services I attended with my Protestant
friends. Touching in their simplicity and with an invariably better-
trained choir, they lacked something all the same—not God, cer-
tainly; maybe Glory.

A letter from my mother, the original convert, arrives here. She
has neither heard nor read the above, but she's received word

through the family grapevine that I'm considering the subject, and she writes to express her views.

> I'm happy to think my non-Catholic background was groundwork for becoming a good Catholic. I wanted to question every aspect and choose the best and eliminate the worst. . . . I like to think people like me are what has brought about changes in the Church. I don't think that [my children] have left the Church—I believe that all are still a part of the Church and maybe they're not practicing but still are members of the Church and treat all people with respect and consideration in their beliefs.

This is the Protestant in my mother speaking—believing that the individual, not the institution, arbitrates what is and is not Catholic; that simple respect and charity are sufficient unto the cause. This, of course, is not the message of the Roman Catholic Church, which understands that it has endured and prospered exactly because it insists on being taken on its own terms.

The Roman Catholic Church *has* changed, of course, as has the South. Hodgenville, the Protestant town across the river, now has its own Roman Catholic church, while in the fervor for the plain and simple that followed Vatican II, the rococo frescoes of St. Catherine's were painted over in an aqua intended to match the Virgin's blue but closer in color to the paint used for swimming pools. Midnight Mass is now at eight P.M., the purple shrouds have gone the way of the Latin Mass.

But in the New Church, in the New South, ways of seeing the world persist long after surfaces have changed. As for me, I seldom go to Mass, and my forays into No-Priest Land led me to subscribe long ago to the essential fact of the Protestant world view: that when push comes to shove, men and women confront their gods and demons alone, without benefit or need of an intermediary. For better or worse, however, I find that I am still affected—or afflicted, depending on one's point of view—with the Catholic way of seeing things, which I have chosen not to reject: an insistence on the primacy of mystery, on the fundamental irrationality of being, on the significance of grace as a force in determining the course of human actions.

For a while, across the river among my Protestant friends, I was afraid that I had been alone in receiving an addictive dose of the opiate of the masses, Roman Catholic–style. Then I left Kentucky and went to other towns on the water, on Midwestern rivers or on the Pacific. There I discovered other Catholics who shared my dilemma, in kind if not in degree. American Roman Catholics, they'd come to their faith in a Protestant land, and had absorbed its influences even as they retained Roman Catholicism's basic view of the universe and humankind's place in it. No doubt this is what makes us so troublesome to Rome.

In my experience—that is to say, an American experience—a parallel leaps here to mind: that of Southern liberals, confronting the land of their birth, a place that shapes, irrevocably, its native sons' and daughters' ways of seeing the world, and yet about which those same persons have such mixed emotions.

I have not lived in the South in years, and I participate in Catholic services only under duress. But I've chosen to keep my accent, as I've chosen to keep the Catholic way of seeing the world. Partly this is in response to others' outspoken perceptions of me, delivered so often that they've acquired the ring of uncomfortable truth: anyone with *that* accent must be a Southerner, anyone *that* guilt-ridden must be a Catholic. More to the point, I think, my choice represents a peculiar, self-conscious decision shared by liberal Southerners and backsliding Catholics everywhere to affirm and preserve our troublesome inheritance.

The Roman Catholic Church does not encourage the bending and cutting of its precepts to individual consciences, any more than that collective understanding we call the South encourages one to claim it as one's own while believing deeply in liberal, humanist ideals. This is how the Church and the South are alike: the proposition they deliver to their own is all or nothing. I think of the Sistine Chapel's flayed self-portrait of Michelangelo, ridden with guilt and hanging from the fingers of St. Bartholomew, and the fierce, self-incriminating denials of Quentin Compson that end Faulkner's *Absalom, Absalom!*: "I dont hate [the South]! I dont hate it!" The great art of the Church, the great literature of the South are often as not born from the dramatic tension inherent in confronting, as art must, this institution, this place that one can neither abandon nor abide.

In thinking of the Church, in thinking of the South, I have come to understand that this is what they share: an uncompromising demand that they be accepted on their terms. It is exactly because they demand our love so wholly and unconditionally that we find them so hard to leave behind, that they draw us back in spite of ourselves. In this age of relativism, few places can, few people do.

Father to the Mother
(1989)

This is what is facing me, a confirmed city boy for eighteen years, as I drive a rented car south from the Louisville airport to the small town where I grew up: a summer with my widowed mother, who lives alone in a house that once supported parents, four daughters, four sons, three dogs, a flock of Rhode Island Reds, a one-acre garden, and two hundred quail that my father brought home from the Rolling Fork Fish & Game Club as an experiment in reestablishing the birds in neighboring fields. For two months before leaving San Francisco I had turned down jobs, weaseled out of meetings, left phone calls unreturned. On my kitchen table I kept a running list of things to do during this three-month visit:

1) replace water heater
2) put on new roof
3) tear out wood-burning stove
4) buy air conditioner (window unit)
5) insulate greenhouse

Youngest son, self-employed, I was the likely candidate for these jobs—and for broaching other matters more delicate:

6) what about money?
7) living alone? Why not a dog?
8) love life?

So I drove up to find my mother sharing the porch swing with a new man (*a new man?*), a longtime friend of the family, an eighty-two-year-old Southern gentleman ten years her senior. "You don't think he's too old for you?" I whispered while he was inside. She shrugged. "He's alive, which gives him an advantage over most men around here." When he returned he put his arm around her, she cuddled up to him. My mother, whom my father hadn't publicly kissed in forty-seven years of marriage!

That Saturday he took my mother and me to the theater (Father hadn't attended a play in his life). Late that night we drove home—the kids (them) in back, the chauffeur (me) up front. At his house I parked in the drive. I waited a few seconds—a thick and delicious moment. Then I cleared my throat. "I think I'll get my sunglasses out of the trunk," I said.

A few weeks later, since fishing is her passion and my mother's friend is no fisherman, I searched out the bamboo poles from the depths of the woodshed. We spent an hour sanding rust from the old hooks. "Every time we fished we had to sand every single one clean," she said. "Father would never throw a one of them away."

We stashed the bank poles in the trunk and drove to the river, where everything was feeding on whatever was in reach: dragonflies, mosquitoes, water snakes on top, bass, catfish, crappie in the sinkholes, and, stalking the mussel beds, the great blue herons. Mother cocked her head, listening. "'Can't catch when the locusts grind,' is what Father always said." But catch we did: the next morning a single pole bobbed and dipped, a nice blue channel cat. Back home she pried the hook free, studied it a moment, then tossed it in the garbage.

Should I dwell on her strength—plunging a butcher knife into the channel cat's steel-gray head—or her need—red-faced with anger at her impotence before the medical bureaucracy? I know what we wanted to hear, I and my scattered brothers and sisters:

she's doing fine, she loves our visits but doesn't need our help, she has her bridge club, bowling, golf, reading, volunteer work, church, friends. Over long-distance lines, in letters she tells us this and we believe her.

But a summer is a long time to keep up an illusion, and one Monday morning after I'd been gone for the weekend she dropped her guard. "It's Sunday afternoons that get to you," she said. "There's nobody to call, nothing on television, a million things you can't bring yourself to do. Sometimes I just get in the car and drive." Then she stood abruptly and disappeared into the house, to reappear a half hour later waving a wrench: "I fixed the toilet," she said. I checked it out: the leak was gone.

I was away from San Francisco for only three months, but things move fast in California—out of sight, out of mind. To listen to my friends, I might have been leaving for Beulah Land. Three months in *Kentucky?* Drop a line, my friends said, and I could have cut their skepticism with a knife. Let us know how it goes, they said, we're thinking of doing the same for our parents.

That's what struck me over the summer, as I typed away in the basement, the only cool place in the house: how many of my peers told me of *their* parents in the same situation—the nuclear family exploded, its children scattered over hundreds or thousands of miles. *The child is father to the man,* I thought, though more often to the woman. All my friends, now parents, had parents, most often widows, most often living alone and at some distance from their offspring, some comfortable, most depending in some measure— financial, emotional—on their children.

About that air conditioner and my list of projects. My mother refused to let me buy a window unit until they went on sale, which they never did in that long hot summer. The weekend we planned to put on a new roof it rained. That same weekend we were supposed to take out the old wood-burning stove. We *did* replace the water heater. Mostly we went on walks. One moment I was teacher, the next I was student. I talked about life in the big city, she taught me the names of birds and plants and the stories that went with them.

On the last evening of my visit we walk through the fields of the nearby Abbey of Gethsemani, where years before she and my father had thrown picnics for monks who sneaked out of the enclosure. In the tolling of Vespers I hear their names, a medieval litany: Clement, Christopher, Alfred, Wilfred, Conrad, Simeon, Fintan, who gave me his name. They are almost all gone now, drawn away by marriage, secular careers, other religious orders, death.

In the fencerows we hear the scratch and scatter of quail—*lots* of quail; a covey explodes under our noses. The summer heat has broken, the paths are lined with fall wildflowers: partridge pea, boneset, goldenrod, ironweed. The sun sets in a hurry, the light is low and autumnal; all around us is the knowing that this, another summer, is coming to an end.

Somehow this one gesture sums up that summer: my mother's hand, wrinkled and spotted with age, stripping a dried stalk of purple loosestrife for seed to plant in her wildflower garden. She is careful to point out, as her hand cups the seed, that she is scattering some for those who come next year.

Basketball Days

(1996)

I came of age in the land where the basketball never stops, in the waning years of the basketball dynasty built by Adolph Rupp and his University of Kentucky Wildcats. Like most of the state I had basketball in my genes—my mother played for her school's girls' team, and my three older brothers for the local Catholic high; my sisters were or tried out to be cheerleaders. On winter nights the family knelt for the rosary—I prayed for our side to win. Afterward we clustered around the radio as Cawood Ledford, the mellifluous voice of Kentucky, called the games on clear-channel WHAS.

Then Louisville television stations boosted their signals over the hilltops, and live broadcasts of Saturday afternoon Southeastern Conference games entered our living rooms. My mother led the family in cheers, shaking pompoms and wearing a UK blue garter as she shouted instructions to Rupp and his team. Whenever the Cats made some spectacular play she hiked the garter higher up her leg; in close games she ran out of thigh and had to start over at her knee.

How we lived for those games! I doubt that any city slicker can grasp the grandness of our obsession, if only because no one who grew up in a city can understand how crushingly dull life can be on a winter afternoon in the country, when the weather is too rugged to go out and for days there has been nothing, nothing to do. In gym class we imagined ourselves playing in UK's Memorial Coliseum, no matter that our gym had a tile floor and a shorter-than-regulation court. As the second-tallest eighth-grader, I had one glorious day—I scored eleven points and blocked two shots, and in a running one-on-one I faked out my taller classmate by stopping dead in midstride. His inertia carried him *splat!*, into the cinderblock wall, while I scored what memory glamorizes as a lay-up.

The coach asked me to try out for the junior high team; I turned him down. By then I'd figured out that the worst epithet the guys in the locker room could hurl was exactly what I longed to do. I'd discovered that the game was, among other things, an invitation to the flesh. Skimpy uniforms, ropy muscles, sweaty bodies—at night I dreamed of Jimmy Duboise, whose left leg was mysteriously, erotically withered and scarred, and who specialized in jump shots from the far corners. He hung suspended in the air long after the ball left his hands, his fingers curled in perfect sendoff form, the ball flew through the hoop, cradled for a split second by the net before dropping through with that cleanest of sounds . . . and there was Jimmy, drawn back to earth, landing casually but carefully on his good leg.

In my dreams I loved him for his wound and he reciprocated in kind. Then I saw him in the locker room and I turned and went the other way. After that year ended, I never played again. Stunned by the power of my desire, aware that it might betray me into ridicule or violence, I took to living less in my body and more in my heart and head; I took to writing stories.

The calendar pages flip by—I'm in my forties now and in suspiciously good shape. Somewhere in my twenties I discovered running and swimming and biking and lifting weights, sports where I was not touching other men; and then—better late than never—I discovered touching men.

A few weeks ago I returned to my childhood home for my mother's eightieth birthday celebration, which coincided with the opening week of the NCAA basketball tournament. Parked with my family in front of the tube, I revisited those particular roots by watching more basketball than I'd seen since I was a kid.

The droopy-drawer uniforms look designed to uglify the game's erotic choreography, but the guys are so much hunkier now that they make up for the sagging shorts. All through that long weekend, I watched with regret those extraordinary bodies in their extraordinary free-form ballet. Memory lives in the body, truth resides in gesture, life turns on something done more often than on something said, and my body holds no memory of hanging in midair. I have the musculature but I lack the grace, and I will never learn it now. Only the young can defy gravity; with time we're all pulled down and back to the earth's embrace. Still: as I sat watching day after day, I took some considerable satisfaction in knowing now what I could not have known in the eighth grade—with that many guys on the court, chances are good that I share with some of them something deeper than a love of the game.

After Shock in San Francisco
(1991)

In my public-transit youth, I called it the 22 Fellini, the crosstown bus that begins at the edge of San Francisco Bay in the industrial flatlands that surround China Basin. From there the bus travels west on Sixteenth Street and north on Fillmore, cutting a sociological cross section of one of the world's more ethnically and culturally diverse populations. It rolls first through neighborhoods of Salvadoran, Guatemalan, and Honduran refugees, documented and otherwise; catches a corner of the city's gay neighborhood; then crosses Market Street, the wide diagonal that divides the city and operates as the main thoroughfare for its burgeoning population of homeless.

From there the bus travels through the remnants of the Western Addition, once largely black, now increasingly gentrified. When it reaches the back side of Pacific Heights, the black and Latina maids descend and elderly white widows board for the precipitous drop to the upscale shopping districts of Union and Chestnut Streets. In the Marina District, the route describes a wide turn on a stretch of Fillmore Street, ending, as it began, on landfill created from the rubble of the 1906 earthquake.

At a certain point after the October 1989 quake, some of the homeless who ride the bus for shelter or distraction and the

women from the projects did not get off on the back side of Pacific Heights. Instead, they rode down to the flats of the Marina,
where they dined on food contributed for earthquake victims by
the gourmet delicatessens and restaurants of Union and Chestnut
Streets. They stocked up on clothes—*nice* clothes—that residents
of the Marina and Cow Hollow and Pacific Heights had pulled
from closets and hung on the storm fences erected around the
Marina Middle School Disaster Relief Center. Laden with clothes
and filled with some of the better food this side of the world has to
offer, they boarded the 22 Fillmore for the journey over the hill to
the poorer parts of town.

Before long, questions arose: Who was taking these clothes?
Why were we feeding people who could have lost nothing in the
quake because, in fact, they had nothing to lose? First the donated
food disappeared, then the clothes, then the hot meals provided
by the Red Cross, then, finally, the homeless and the poor. But
their memory remains in the Marina, as vivid as the vacant lots
and cracked walls: a reminder of life on the edge, in this most pre-
cariously poised of American cities; a testimonial to the fragility
of the social contract and technological infrastructure that bind
modern cities together, and to the ways in which, in San Francisco
at least, the forces of nature are working to break that contract.

*

Since the population explosion attendant on the gold rush, San
Franciscans have had a problem that the relatively mild-mannered
quake of October 1989 only underscored: there are too many of
us crammed into a site that should never have been occupied in
the first place. Built virtually overnight in the mid-nineteenth century at the height of America's self-assurance, San Francisco is
among our most outstanding case studies of the long-term implications of Western civilization's confidence in its ability to triumph
over nature.

New York took two centuries to reach a population of 150,000;
San Francisco took twenty-five years and shows it. With every

spectacular view it presents evidence of its builders' indifference to geography, geology, topography: the grid of narrow streets, the jumble of fire-prone houses, the fragility of the water supply, piped two hundred miles from Yosemite National Park and stored in a reservoir created by a dam thrown across the nearest valley—conveniently created by the San Andreas Fault. "Shocking in its obstinate abstraction," Simone de Beauvoir wrote of the city. "The blueprint seems to have been put on paper without the architect ever having seen the site."

The city sits at the tip of a peninsula squeezed between two of the world's most active earthquake faults. To the west, the San Andreas Fault dives into the Pacific just south of the city limits. To the east, the Hayward Fault forms, more or less, the base of the thickly populated Berkeley Hills. In 1836 and 1838, San Francisco experienced earthquakes similar in magnitude to the October 1989 quake, and again in 1865 and 1868. Then in 1906 came "The Big One," which released so much energy geologists generally credit it with "de-stressing" northern California faults for more than seventy years. During those years, the city rebuilt and its suburbs expanded over the fault lines themselves.

All evidence indicates that this period of quiescence has ended. In the decade prior to 1989, northern California has experienced four quakes of 5.5 magnitude or greater on the Richter scale, with the October 1989 quake only the most severe. On top of these mini-quakes, one must bear in mind another of the ironies of life in this lovely place that sets it apart from other earthquake-prone cities: the sources of its particular beauty and charm abet its periodic destruction. From its inception, San Francisco has been built to burn.

Gray Brechin, a San Francisco architectural historian, points out that in most cities of the American West, houses are by and large detached. But San Francisco is built predominantly of row houses, which give it its urbane feel. Cover that wood with paint—more reflective and with a far greater range of colors than brick or masonry—and the result is a pastel stage-set of a city, which to a fire looks like one vast lot of cheek-by-jowl kindling, nicely aged, with fireproofing the exception rather than the rule.

The city burned six times between 1849 and 1852 and again, most disastrously, after the quake of 1906. By then, downtown had been reconstructed in fire-resistant brick, masonry, and steel, but that proved meaningless in the face of broken water mains, broken gas lines, and the flames encroaching from the wood-frame structures that, then as now, surrounded the Financial District.

The calendar pages flip by: it's 5:04 P.M., October 17, 1989. Moderate by the standards of 1906 and centered much farther from the city limits, this quake caused astonishing disruption: The city's emergency hotline went down. Confounding engineers' predictions, a section of the Bay Bridge collapsed. In neighborhoods built on landfill, gas and water mains broke—the same combination that led to the 1906 fire and that will recur in every sizable quake. Meanwhile, many small fires went unattended as the city's firefighting force concentrated on a single Marina District blaze, which they brought under control only when the city's fireboat arrived to pump water from the Bay—the fireboat that, due to budget cuts, had been scheduled to be mothballed at the year's end.

All San Franciscans are aware of some of this; some are aware of all of it and a good deal more. The cumulative effect of this knowledge, exacerbated by the unnerving, continuing aftershocks from the 1989 quake, is a state that one observer compared to the combination of bright chatter and tight-lipped nonchalance that fills airplanes shortly before takeoff. We all know the odds, and the odds on this particular flight on this particular day are pretty good, but they are odds, after all, and in San Francisco, in northern California, there are plenty of knowledgeable people publicly questioning how good they are.

This schizophrenic conflict between knowledge and denial— the certainty of the inevitable, and the need to go on—is characteristic of contemporary life; consider our anemic response to climate change. But in San Francisco we are playing out that conflict with impressive vividness in our struggle to deal, or not to deal, with life on the fault line.

*

After the destruction of 1906, with the city a virtual tabula rasa, a "Citizens' Committee" undertook to impose on the devastated site a street plan adapted from a design completed a year earlier by architect Daniel H. Burnham, a prime mover behind the City Beautiful movement. Wider streets would not only improve the city's aesthetics, the plan's supporters argued, they would aid in combatting fire. "If we trust to individual effort, we will, of course, have an accidental growth, a dangerous growth, so far as fire is concerned," wrote Francis Newlands, a Nevada senator, in his argument for federal support for the plan.

But reconfiguring the city to take its geology and topography into account would have required time and money from a financially strapped city interested in resuming the appearance of normalcy as quickly as possible, so as to avoid the impression that investment here entailed greater than usual risks. In that November's election, the Citizens' Committee plan lost resoundingly. San Francisco was rebuilt on virtually the same lines as before.

In California, in the West, housing patterns reflect our refusal to submit to nature's dictates. Developers build on fault lines, on cliffs, on landfill—until the quake, or fire, or landslide, enters to remind us who's really boss in the wild, wild West. Gradually, the consequences of our hubris are sinking in. "Quake-proof" quietly passed out of California's engineers' parlance sometime after the 1971 Los Angeles San Fernando Valley quake; now the phrase of choice is "quake-resistant." We have thrust our deciduous roots into the soil and struck rock, even as the bay sparkles like mica, the fog rolls over Twin Peaks, and gulls and pelicans wheel and turn under the sheer cliffs at Lands End. A continent is not so much meeting the ocean as throwing itself headlong into the sea, and we are permitted the privilege of witnessing the act.

Except that, in San Francisco, to witness is also to participate. The question San Franciscans, Californians, Westerners are facing, that has been there all along, that is brought to the forefront by quakes, droughts, landslides, fires, is this: Are we willing to accommodate our lives to the limits that the landscape imposes on our presence?

*

"Earthquake love," they called it after the quake of 1906—a phenomenon described by philosopher William James, who was teaching at Stanford that spring, as a euphoria among survivors, "a kind of uplift in the sense of a 'common lot' that [takes] away the sense of loneliness that gives the sharpest edge to the more usual kind of misfortune that may befall a man." After the 1989 quake, there was an unparalleled outpouring of earthquake love, by no means limited to those who experienced the quake. Donations poured in from around the country and the world.

In part, these arose out of the national fascination with San Francisco. America's most popular vacation city, it exists in two dimensions: the city in fact—once first, then second, then third, now fourth in size among California cities—locked in a struggle to maintain its viability as a cultural and economic hub; and the city in memory and imagination, constructed piecemeal from postcards and vacationers' snapshots, but no less a factor in its image of itself than its real-life counterpart.

But earthquake love arises as well from the fear—by no means limited to San Francisco—that our industrialized, technocratic house of cards might someday collapse. To acknowledge that something as apparently solid as terra firma itself can move, violently and without warning, is to call into question the illusion of security and certainty at the heart of our national aspirations. The quake's greatest damage, after all, was not in San Francisco but in the communities—Santa Cruz, Watsonville—located closer to the epicenter. But no one, least of all the television crews, could resist the contrast between the Marina's flawlessly topiaried streets and its crumpled houses, while in the distance the twin deco sculptures of the Golden Gate Bridge towers floated serenely against a brilliant blue sky.

Chicken or egg: Do people live in San Francisco because they live for the moment, or does the city impose that way of living on its residents? A bit of trivia relevant to the question: the city has one of the highest percentage of renters of any American city—

more than 65 percent. Partly this is a function of exorbitant housing costs, but partly it's because this is a city of people who choose to concern themselves with today's concert or meal or view instead of tomorrow's mortgage payment—or earthquake.

In her essay "Notes from a Native Daughter," Joan Didion wrote,

> California is a place where a boom mentality and a sense of Chekhovian loss meet in uneasy suspension; in which the mind is troubled by some buried but ineradicable suspicion that things had better work here, because here, beneath that immense bleached sky, is where we run out of continent.

The twenty-plus years since Didion's essay have revealed what we ought, perhaps, to have known all along but were too busy exploiting a continent to heed: under this immense bleached sky, things work about as well as several thousand years of recorded history might have led us to expect of human nature, and that, if San Francisco's preparation for and response to its earthquake-laden history is any indication, is not very well at all.

The question is not what we can do to prepare for the future but what we are willing to do; and this is not a question that Americans in general and Californians in particular have ever been especially interested in asking. "This is a problem with American psychology," said Raymond J. Brady, director of research for the Association of Bay Area Governments. "We wait until we're torpedoed, then ask how big the hole is. . . . That's a cultural trait of a society that's been relatively affluent and without space limitations. We could always move to somewhere else. Why worry about next year?" Why indeed, except that this is San Francisco, where there is no more space and where, so far as the earthquake is concerned, next year was last year but with more to come.

*

At 5:12 A.M. on April 18, 1991, a band of some two hundred gathers in the city's Financial District for the annual commemoration of the anniversary of the 1906 quake. It's all so very small town, in this city with imperial aspirations: The St. Francis Hook and Ladder Society serves Bloody Marys, certificates are handed out to some ten or fifteen survivors of 1906, we bow our heads to pray, the emcee muffs his lines, the guest of honor never appears, a woman dressed in vaguely Victorian costume steps to the mike to lead us, off-key, in singing "San Francisco." The survivors tell their stories in age-tremulous voices. Afterward we file into a nearby bank where pastries and coffee are being served amid enlarged photographs of the city after the quake and fire.

So we're standing around wishing we were still in bed, when there's a rumble and jolt. The light fixtures sway, a bank guard dives under the nearest teller's desk. Lacking desks, the rest of us freeze—for one, two, three seconds; then it's over, for this time. "Really, this is too much," someone mutters, heading for the door, but the rest of us do what you have to do: we laugh and turn, with a sense of purpose now, to our Bloody Marys.

People are always in danger of being done in by our own myths, but nowhere is that more true than in California, the American myth factory. For better and worse, we are convinced of our ability to outwit nature, or, barring that, of our particular ability to survive, and to improve ourselves in the process. "My first reaction was bitterness," one Marina survivor said. "If we did our civic duty we'd bulldoze the neighborhood into the bay. But now I'm glad because it changed my life. . . . It made me understand the transiency of things."

If this sounds like a bad California joke, stop a moment to consider: Is there, finally, a choice, here or anywhere else? There is a great deal to be learned from an earthquake, after all. This will sound crazy to Easterners—it sounds crazy to many Californians. But there's an experience of force, of power, on a scale vaster than the imagination can comprehend: the infinitesimally short pause beforehand, that split moment (far too short to do anything about it) when the quake veteran knows that the earth is about to roll over in its sleep; the first chatterings of pots and pans and glass, followed by roll and toss as waves of pure energy move through the fluid earth; that unearthly rumble, that incomparable growl, which provides a bass drone to the high-pitched clatter of the pots and the tumble and crash of breaking glass; the rush of adrenalin as, for ten seconds or twenty or (God forbid!) thirty or more, time suspends itself and you clutch uselessly at doorways and pray. Life is reduced to a question of survival, no less, no more.

This is a revelatory state, not so easily induced among prosperous Americans, and—writing as one of the fortunate—not so unfortunately come by. "You were lucky," a friend insists, repeating a refrain heard throughout the days after the quake and into the present: "I was lucky," "We were lucky," "San Francisco was lucky." No doubt about it—but then most of us were, most of us are, most of the time.

In Flannery O'Connor's short story "A Good Man Is Hard to Find," The Misfit says of the grandmother, "She would have been a good woman, if it had been somebody there to shoot her every minute of her life." The Misfit is a philosopher who explains the phenomenon of this city, which has made it at once the butt of too many jokes, the nation's favorite escape, and—perhaps a metaphor for the rest of the planet: we're all artists and philosophers here, living with the gun that we ourselves have loaded, and making it up as we go.

Part II

Journals of the Plague Years
(2016)

In my late twenties and throughout my thirties, fate placed me in the midst of the AIDS epidemic in San Francisco, arguably the world's hardest-hit city in those first years because of its compact size, its relatively large gay population, and its history of sexual liberation. The gay writers of that era were the bridge between a generation for whom writing for mainstream publications required remaining in the closet, and a generation of openly gay men and women who have risen to editorial and political power. I was born to the generation in between—the generation that made that change possible—though to give fate its due, AIDS gave us little choice: silence equaled death.

More than once I transgressed my publishers' boundaries around writing about the literal facts of sexual desire. As I was coming out in the late 1970s—brought out, in fact, by the successful fight against California's 1978 Briggs Initiative, which proposed banning not only gay teachers but any mention of homosexuality in the classroom—I was witness to the emergence of ways of life and love that had not been acknowledged, much less celebrated, since the earliest civilizations.

But writing about that culture ran up against a stone wall of prudery and homophobia. Few West Coast and no mainstream

East Coast publications were willing to acknowledge the existence of same-gender desire. Most notoriously, *New York Times* executive editor A. M. Rosenthal would not allow the word "gay" in print even in direct quotation. So a community of readers and writers grew up around pages passed from hand to hand, a publishing subculture of small magazines that grew larger and glossier as advertisers discovered a market but were still available only via subscription—their covers concealed in brown paper wrappers—or in gay bookstores, which sprang up and thrived by serving this niche market.

AIDS changed all that. In 1989, when I published my first column in the *New York Times Magazine*, the nation's premier newspaper had not yet overcome its resistance to writing about AIDS. Its editors and journalists—more than a few gay men and lesbians among them—were not permitted to reference or describe the gay subculture that was bearing the brunt of the illness. Writing about AIDS without writing about the subculture it affected produced weirdly strained prose. In his heart-breaking essay/memoir on the subject, published in November 1990 in the *Times Magazine* as he was dying, *Times* staffer Larry Josephs was still not allowed to provide a context for his death—to reference how he contracted the disease, to mention his caregivers, to describe community activists' desperate fight to bring the disease and the government's indifference to public attention.

Then *Times* staffers began literally collapsing on the job. Anger in the newsroom grew, in the face of the reality that every other major newspaper in the country was providing front-page coverage of the topic, as ACT UP's media-savvy protests disrupted services at St. Patrick's, blocked the Golden Gate Bridge, and drew television cameras to the blood-spattered doors of the National Institutes of Health.

From the time of my first publication in the *Times Magazine* ("How I Spent My Summer Vacation," included here as "Father to the Mother"), I was dogged by a visceral certainty that I was destined to play a role in breaking that news barrier. I remained at home rather than joining the street protests because, I told myself, the pen was my tool and I was more useful at the desk than in the streets. Across those months of vocal protest and activism I waited and watched for the story that would be my means to undermine the status quo. In this I was hardly alone—the *Times* was a barn door of a target—but Rosenthal's power was so complete that it was clear that the catalysts for change would have to come from outside.

Then my partner Larry Rose died of AIDS in Paris in October 1990—a story I have told at length in *Geography of the Heart: A Memoir*. In March 1991, I went to visit Larry's parents at their bungalow in Santa Monica, California. Moments after I entered the room, I heard the quite literal voice of some small writing angel: *This is it*. At the evening's end, sitting in my rental car outside the Rose home, I turned on the dome light and wrote "The Limitless Heart" on the back of my rental contract. The column ran in the *Times Magazine* on June 23, 1991—to my knowledge, the paper's first affirmative mention of same-gender love.

Six months later, in response to overwhelming pressure from within and without, the *Times* moved Rosenthal upstairs and gave him a twice-weekly column. Overnight the *Times* did an about-face. An anecdote illustrates the transformation: In 1990, in publishing "The Limitless Heart," my *Times* editors forbade me the use of the word "lover" to describe my partner. Two years later, confronted with an avalanche of hostile mail in response to the same-gender lovemaking mentioned in my next column, "Lucky Fellow," those same editors printed a single response—from a gay man who took me to task for not having the courage to use the word "lover." Happy to have played a role in turning the wheel of change, grateful at the opportunity to restore the proper word, I use it in those essays reprinted here.

Visiting Paris in 1994, I spoke with a San Francisco journalist who had moved to Europe, and who asked me for news of the epidemic back home. My report, he said, reminded him of his interviews with Bosnian widows, refugees from that especially brutal war, who did not want to talk to outsiders because only those who had lived through the experience could appreciate its horror.

These journals of the plague years act, I hope, as an homage to
that era of terror and heartbreak and death and anger and love.

The Limitless Heart
(1991)

It is late March—the Saturday of Passover 1991 to be exact—and I am driving an oversized rental car through west Los Angeles. This side of the city I have never seen except in the company of my lover Larry Rose, who died of AIDS in a Paris hospital some six months earlier.

He was an only child, who asked more than once that I promise to visit his parents after his death. Youngest son of a large family and a believer in brutal honesty, I'd refused. I have too much family already, I told him. There are limits to how much love I can give.

Now I am driving along one of the lovelier streets of Santa Monica, San Vicente Boulevard, west from Wilshire to the Pacific. The street is divided by a broad green median lined with coral trees, which the city has seen fit to register as landmarks. They spread airy, elegant crowns against a movie-set heaven, a Maxfield Parrish blue. Each branch bleeds at its tip an impossibly scarlet blossom, as if the limbs themselves had pierced the thin-skinned sky.

Larry's parents, Fred and Kathy Rose, are too old to get about much. They are German Jews who spent the war years hiding in a Dutch village a few miles from Germany itself. Beaten by Nazis before the war, Fred hid for three years with broken vertebrae, unable to see a doctor. When he was no longer able to move, Kathy descended to the street to find help, to see falling from the sky the parachutes of their liberators. After the war they married and came to California, promised land of this promised land. Like Abraham and Sarah, in their advanced years they had a single son—proof that it is possible, in the face of the worst, to pick up sticks and start again.

Fred greets me at the door of their small bungalow. Even now, after dinner, he wears his customary suit and tie, but he seems smaller than in my earlier visits. In his bent and shrunken frame I understand how Larry was a shield against his memories, and now Larry is gone.

Fred, Kathy, and I sit to talk, but Fred is reserved; he does not talk about Larry with the women of his life—his wife or his surviving sister. No doubt he fears giving way before his grief, and his life has not allowed for much giving way. This much he and I share: a gay man who grew up in the rural South, I am no stranger to hiding.

Kathy always goes to bed early—partly by way of coping with grief—but this evening Fred all but asks her to retire. After she leaves, he begins talking of Larry, and I listen and respond with gratefulness. We are two men in control, who permit ourselves to speak to each other of our loss because we subscribe implicitly, jointly, unconditionally to this code of conduct.

Fred tells a familiar story, of the day when Larry, then eight years old, wanted to go fishing. The quintessential urban Jew, Fred nonetheless bought poles and hooks and drove fifty miles to Laguna Beach. There they dropped their lines from a pier to discover the hooks dangled some ten feet above the water. "Thank God," Fred says. "Otherwise we might have caught something." A passerby scoffed—"What the hell do you think you're trying to catch?" Fred shrugged, unperturbed. "Flying fish," he said.

I respond with my most vivid memory of my time with Larry. A wiser man than I, he spoke many times of his great luck, his great good fortune. "I'm so lucky," he said again and again. Denial pure and simple, or so I told myself in our first years together. AZT, ddI, ACT UP, CMV, DHPG, and what I came to think of as the big "A" itself—he endured this acronymed life, while I listened and participated and helped when I could.

Until our third and final trip to Paris, when on our last night to walk about the city we sat in the courtyard of the Picasso Museum. There under a dusk-deep sky I turned to him and said, "I'm so lucky," and it was as if the time allotted to him to teach me this lesson, the time allotted to me to learn it, had been consumed, and there was nothing left but the facts of things to play out.

A long pause after this story—I have ventured beyond what I permit myself, what I am permitted.

I change the subject, asking Fred to talk of the war years. He speaks not of his beating or of murdered family and friends but of moments of affection, loyalty, even humor, until he speaks of winters spent confined to bed, huddled in Kathy's arms, their breaths freezing on the quilt as they sang together to pass time, to stay warm, to distract him from his pain, to ward off their fear.

Another silence. Now he has ventured too far. "I have tried to forget these stories," he says in his halting English.

In the presence of these extremes of love and sorrow I am reduced to cliché. "It's only by remembering them that we can hope to avoid repeating them," I say.

"They are being repeated all the time," Fred says. "It is bad sometimes to watch too much television. You see these things and you know we have learned nothing."

Are we so dense that we can learn nothing from all this pain, all this death? Is it impossible to learn from experience? The bitterness of these questions I can taste, as I drive east to spend the night at a relative's apartment.

Just south of the seedier section of Santa Monica Boulevard I stop at a bar recommended by a friend. I need a drink, I need the company of men like me—survivors, for the moment anyway, albeit of a very different struggle.

The bar is filled with Latino drag queens wearing extraordinary clothes. Eighty years of B movies have left Hollywood the nation's most remarkable supply of secondhand dresses, many of which, judging from this evening, have made their ways to these men's closets.

I am standing at the bar, very Anglo, very butch, very out of place, very much thinking of leaving, when a tiny, wizened, gray-haired Latina approaches the stage, where under jerry-built lights (colored cellophane, Scotch tape) a man lip-synchs to Brazilian rock. His spike heels raise him to something more than six feet; he wears a floor-length sheath dress slit up the sides and so taut, so brilliantly silver, so lustrous that it catches and throws back the faces of his audience. The elderly Latina raises a dollar bill. On tottering heels he lowers himself, missing not a word of his song while half-crouching, half-bending so that she may tuck her dollar in his cleavage and kiss his cheek. "*Su abuelita,*" the bartender says. "His grandmother."

One A.M. in the City of Angels—the streets are clogged with cars. Stuck in traffic, I am haunted by voices and visions: by the high, thin songs of Fred and Kathy as they huddle under their frozen quilt, singing into their breaths; by a small boy and his father sitting on a very long pier, their baitless fishhooks dangling above the vast Pacific; by the face of su abuelita, uplifted and adoring, mirrored in her grandson's dress.

Somewhere a light changes, the traffic unglues itself. As cars begin moving, I am visited by two last ghosts—Larry Rose and me, sitting in the courtyard of the Hôtel Salé, transfigured by the limitless heart.

Lucky Fellow
(1993)

Across the second year after Larry's death, I became friends with Mark, a man whose lover of a decade had been dying for more than two years. On Mark's birthday, a year or so after we met, I call and offer him these options: coming to my place for lunch; going out for lunch, my treat. He chooses my place, which on that particular Friday carries some sad and delicious possibility of making love.

I am cheered by the prospect of leaving off work to spend a Friday afternoon with drop-dead handsome Mark. In conversation we never talk of our lovers, dying or dead, but we'd established that we are each HIV-negative and that it had been at least two years since Mark had made love and longer for me—in the last months before my lover Larry's death, he'd grown too weak to make love. In our mutual caregiving Mark and I had carefully avoided talk of the future, content with holding another person's commiserating hand—though the hand-holding had been mostly metaphorical, both of us being caught up in that man thing and, after years of living-with-dying, very much into guarding our hearts.

So I go out and buy birthday candles and a couple of chocolate cupcakes and a book for a gift, and come home and wrap the book and set the table and stick the candles in the cupcakes and take a shower.

And I'm climbing from the shower and searching for a clean pair of Calvin Kleins when the phone rings and it's Mark, saying that his lover has just got the results from his latest test and it's *Pneumocystis* again, and his doctor has exhausted all drugs to treat it and doesn't know what he can do, and Mark wants to spend the afternoon consoling his lover over this grim turn of events. I make some comments I hope are supportive, then I hang up and get dressed (the ragged old Fruit of the Looms will do) and eat my bowl of soup and one of the chocolate cupcakes and resign myself to resuming work.

But as I sit to my work the phone rings again, and it's Mark, saying that the doctor had called back to say he's heard about an experimental drug that only kills 10 percent of the people who take it, and he's sending it over to start Mark's lover on it right away. And since for the moment Mark's lover is feeling OK and since it *is* Mark's birthday, maybe he *will* come over for lunch. So he does in fact come over and I feed him soup and light the candles on the remaining cupcake. He carves it in two and gives me half, and in his gesture I understand what we both want: that short triumph over fate, over time and memory and history, that desire might bring at its best.

And on that day desire turns out to be very much at its best. The old confusion of love and sex and death carried (safely) to the limit; a modest act of defiance, a declaration of life, thumbing our noses in the face of the beast.

Then I take Mark's hand and he takes it back and pulls on his clothes and goes home to his dying lover.

*

I visit Bill, a friend whose lover had died a few months before my lover and who is HIV-positive. His disease has progressed rapidly since the last time I'd seen him, to the point where he's lost his sight to the same opportunistic infection I'd once feared would blind my lover.

I arrive just as Bill is sitting to an unhappily familiar routine—administering his daily IV treatment. His sister brings him the medical equipment, while I choose some music—Natalie Cole. Bill insists on hooking up by himself the IV pump that delivers drugs to a catheter concealed under his shirt. But he can't see well enough to locate the catheter with the needle, and his sister comes to help. She tries to hook up the needle and pricks her finger.

A moment of dreadful silence, in which we all think about the plague, and how it's spread, and what a tragedy it would be if Bill's sister, who has come across the continent to care for her brother, were somehow to contract the disease in her caregiving.

I'd watched my lover do this, I know how the IV works; I know that the needle with which she's stuck herself is not the needle that feeds into her brother's bloodstream but the needle that fits into his external catheter. The chances of her having infected herself from such a needle stick are virtually nonexistent—the needle with which she's stuck herself had never been in direct contact with Bill's blood. But the unhappy possibility rears its head all the same. She hurries to the kitchen. Bill calls after her to wash the wound with iodine. I rise to pick up some medical paraphernalia Bill's sister had dropped, to get her blood on my hand. I stare at my hand.

We all pretend this isn't happening, or if it is happening, that it really doesn't matter. I drop the bloodied paraphernalia in the trash can. The sister returns from washing her hands and shrugs with affected unconcern. "No big deal," she says.

I know how the disease can and can't be spread; I know the odds. But I'm a white, more-or-less prosperous American man, so used to the assumption of predictability and security that I don't even know I assume it. I'm a child of the Enlightenment, inheritor and purveyor of a culture that assumes that everything can or will be explained and controlled. I've surrounded myself with gadgets (flip a switch, push a button) that demonstrate how completely I control the world. Then chance, circumstance, luck—call it what I want—enters my life in any of its infinite guises and I'm disoriented and distraught. I've been so oblivious to any reminder of life's nonstop tenuousness.

Bill gets his catheter to drip correctly. Natalie Cole launches into "Unforgettable." We settle into a tinny, bright conversation.

*

My first date, two years after my lover's death: I'd met a landscape architect who lives in the East Bay, whom I invite to the theater. I cross the Bay Bridge to Oakland, where a full moon rises above hills burned clear in the firestorm that swept through in autumn 1991. Tom, my date, is a nice-looking guy with a steady paycheck—every writer's fantasy. When he tells me he's *reading a novel*, I'm impressed and for a long minute bedeviled by stupid, involuntary fantasies of a partner, someone to fill this void left by my lover's death.

And then through the evening, no mention of his long-term plans; none of the casual references to the future that pepper our conversations and of which we're not even aware, and all the while that dark knowledge growing larger and more unavoidable.

Then it's after the play, he's driving me back to my car, and the air is charged with possibility. Never good at leaving well enough alone, I break the silence by asking what he's reading, which turns out to be Stephen King, but that's OK, I don't hold it against him. "I'm an Anne Rice fan myself," I say—a small enough lie for a first date. From vampire novels I make an easy conversational leap to complaining about the mess of blackberry briars my landlord calls a yard.

"What you need is a landscape architect," Tom says.

"We'll both be old men before I can afford you," I say.

An awkward pause. Tom clears his throat. "There's something you ought to know," he says, but I've figured it out already, I don't need to be told and I don't want to hear it. I cover his free hand with mine. "Next date," I say.

And then I'm homeward bound after a chaste peck on the cheek from Tom, but the heart's landscape wants company and so I drive not west across the Bay Bridge but east into the burned and blackened Oakland hills. There I park on some fire-ravaged lane and step from the car. No houses or trees are left to block the view—the long bridge, the dark mass of Yerba Buena Island rising from the bay's black mirror, the city's glittering towers. The full moon paints the ash-covered earth in whiteface.

I walk up a driveway leading past the mangled remains of a mailbox to a rectangular hole—the foundation of someone's life. I look across the bay and in bitterness I think, *The best gays and lesbians can hope for from mainstream religion is to be left alone, but we all need somebody, the earth needs somebody in these tough times to hold up some light, to say yes, death comes but it's part of the great cycle, how can we know love without knowing loss, there is joy in accepting the mystery in which we're immersed.* And I'd set out to learn these things, and a time had arrived when I could think, *Yes, that's right, I'm getting it.* And then someone like Tom appears in my life and everything about his grace and beauty and infection says, *Find some joy here, dolt.*

I think about all this and all I can manage is a sad smile, a reaction I couldn't explain then and can't explain now, but the next day when I mention it to a straight friend from the suburbs, he looks at me as if I'm losing my mind. And maybe I am; or is this just the difference between those inside the epidemic and those looking on? What have I been brought to? "The lucky fellow," Elie Wiesel writes of the terrorist leader in *Dawn*. "At least he can cry. When a man weeps he knows that one day he will stop."

The Secret Decoder Ring Society
(2016)

This particular chapter of the novel I call my life begins as I'm
searching through old photographs for relics to contribute to an
album being assembled for a friend's fiftieth birthday. I know and
admire people who mount their photos in albums carefully labeled
with year and location, but I look at mine once or twice when
they come back from the developer for the vicarious thrill (I was
there? Doing *that?*), then I toss them in a jumble into a box labeled
"PIX," which over the years has become five boxes.

What wells up from the Pleistocene of my past is a photo of
five men in our prime—handsome city bucks, clean-cut and buff,
gathered on the prow of a small sailboat on San Francisco Bay
and wearing bright seagoing colors. I'm clutching a bottle of
Veuve Clicquot—we might be on a Sunday lark, but in fact we
are scattering the ashes of our friend Salvador Franco. I will name
those men—from left to right: Fred Rosenberg, Mike O'Neill, me,
Steven Rosen, and Todd Venema—and so return them to life,
however briefly, for they are all dead except me. Missing from the
photo but always present to me: Larry Rose, whom I had met at
Salvador's memorial service the day before, and with whom I will
share just over three too-brief years before he dies, teaching me in
the process that love does not measure itself by clock and calendar

(does a mother love her child less because it is young?) but is our entryway into the true world, shorn of the illusions of time and space.

I have not yet read a full accounting of those terrible, transcendent years. First there were the angry, bitter, groundbreaking books of Paul Monette. In 1996, Mark Doty's elegy *Heaven's Coast* and Bernard Cooper's incisive *Truth Serum* appeared simultaneously with my *Geography of the Heart*—all three books by HIV-negative survivors trying to construct some kind of meaning from the rubble.

But all three writers focus on particular stories, and though our wounds have made us wise beyond our years we haven't yet the perspective to tally the devastation. The project wants a scholar's labor combined with an artist's discerning eye. Even so, the story of those times may withstand any power but that of metaphor—of fiction—of poetry—for how does one describe what has never been known? How can we measure the impact of all those lives lost, cut short, men and women dead in their forties, their thirties, their twenties, their teens, as children?

*

The early years—1984 through 1989—were the hardest. We had no knowledge of the disease, none, and no drugs to treat it. Every day brought cases of new, ever-stranger forms of opportunistic infections in yet another friend. Doctors were playing whack-a-mole with people's lives—address the skin boils only to find rampant thrush in the mouth and elsewhere, and what's going on with this neuropathy? The earliest manifestations were disfiguring—Kaposi's sarcoma, with its ugly purple lesions covering the body—and they were bad enough, but then sometime in the mid-1980s CMV-induced blindness and AIDS-related dementia made themselves known. Doctors who had emerged fresh-scrubbed and optimistic from medical school, eager to be heroes or heroines, found themselves with practices where sixty, seventy, eighty per cent of their patients were dying or dead and there was nothing, nothing to be done. Day by day friends were going slowly blind and slowly insane, and still there was nothing to be done, and still it was not at all clear that caring for them was not an invitation to contracting the virus, and still it was true that, though there was heroism and self-sacrifice, one motivation for the caregivers was that tomorrow we might find ourselves stricken in the same way—or worse—and caregiving was a bet against the future, a prayer that someone would care for us as we had cared for others.

Finally, in the late 1980s, antiviral drugs began to appear, most notably AZT, but no one knew the appropriate dosage and the dying became guinea pigs on which the dosage was worked out. People sickened and died of AZT poisoning, but faced with horrific alternatives on all sides, who wanted to take the risk of reducing the dosage of the only drug available?

*

I will give voice to a charming, unspoken secret—I will point to the elephant in our midst. The radicals on the right wing are correct, have always been correct: the arts really are the province of the wounded, chief among them Jews, homosexuals, racial minorities, the poor, and women. I am not, of course, excluding the contribution of Anglo heterosexual men, only offering a generalization true, so far as I can tell, for at least the last century and arguably before. Senator Jesse Helms understood this fact in launching his vituperative attack on the National Endowment for the Arts. His predecessor in spirit, Senator Joseph McCarthy, singled out communists; Senator Helms, nobody's dummy, understood that communist-baiting was passé, that he needed to work other, more hard-wired veins of prejudice to exploit the majority's fear of the wounded, its fear of those who have been singled out for testing by fate. Fear, and hatred—for what is the latter but the acting out of the former?

Fast forward, and I'm befriended by two Franciscan friars at San Francisco International Airport, where we strike up a conversation while waiting for our bags. They're old-school religious, a

tall serious Irishman and a short plump Italian, Boston boys who
have dedicated their lives to the poor and oppressed—the living
definition of Christians. The Italian makes bitter jokes about Pope
Benedict XVI's Gucci glasses and Prada shoes ("What kind of
queen does he think he is?") while the Irishman, the more reticent
blood of the north in his veins, nods but holds his tongue. They
tell these jokes to me, a stranger, because they have recognized
me as a fellow traveler in ways for which there are no frequent
flier miles, only the companionship of the oppressed, the bond of
shared membership in the secret decoder ring society.

Does our unspoken, keenly understood fellowship arise because
its endurance over centuries gives lie to the illusions of power?
The machinations of the Medici are lost to all but specialists, while
everyone recognizes the names of the artists they patronized, so
many of whom were people loving people of the same gender.

Why does power fear and hate beauty? The rich and powerful
endow museums, less that the public may encounter the pleasure
and stimulation of art than to associate their names with the immortality that is said to accompany it. Experience and my mother
have taught me that envy is the foundation for oppression—the
suits' envy of the life that language in its wisdom long ago labeled
"gay"; the law's envy of the heart that so freely gives itself in love. I
did not choose to be gay, but I did choose to ally myself with those
who find beauty in suffering—the wisest act of my life thus far.

And now Pope Benedict announces that, having taken fifteen
hundred years to stop persecuting the Jews, the Roman Catholic
Church will turn its attention to homosexuals. May God save us
from what he calls compassion.

All That Is Human Is Mine
(1996)

In twenty-plus years as a citizen of San Francisco, I never lived in the Castro. The closest I got was a high-ceilinged flat at Eighteenth and Guerrero in the mid-1980s, five blocks and in those days cultural light years removed from the gay ghetto.

My decision to live in other neighborhoods grew partly from circumstance—the Castro never offered me a place that met a writer's requirements of peace and affordability. But the Castro was never my neighborhood of choice. In those days it did not offer me much promise as the foundation of an enduring community; as often as I visited, and much as I felt at home in the city as a whole, I never felt at home there. Raised in the rural, matriarchal South, I knew what constituted home, and it did not include a neighborhood where women, when present, were relegated to the margins, or the practice of "fluff and turn," in which a speculator bought a house, slapped on a coat of paint, and moved out a year later, selling at a 25 percent markup. Yes, the sex-and-drugs scene was a celebration of breaking down gay mens' closet doors, but after a few high-speed years it frayed about the edges—too many men (I have been among them) searching for love and community in the wrong places, unwilling to acknowledge that, even apart from the arrival of HIV, the party really had gone on too long.

These were the Castro's darkest years—the early- to mid-1980s, after the arrival of AIDS but before the rise of the hospice and HIV patient advocacy movements.

But then a miracle happened: the neighborhood rose to the challenge, in countless acts of courage whose collective impact continues to shape our lives—to offer one example, the hospice practices that we adopted and refined transformed physicians from deities to caregivers. The creation of something from nothing is the unique province of the divine; in forging a community where none existed, and with no template to guide us, the men and women of the Castro came as close to the expression of divinity as any person might expect. The men and women, brothers and sisters who were ill or who have died and the people who cared for them offer a lesson in how death is not to be feared but accepted as the left-side companion to light and life, which we must acknowledge and respect if we are to be fully alive.

I write from exile—teaching in New York—but I close my eyes against the light skating off the Hudson and it all comes back: Friday afternoons at the inimitable Café Flore. The men who loved me for a night, for a life. The motorcyclist I saw struck and killed at the intersection of Castro and Market, an instant and terrible memento mori. My first HIV test at the Seventeenth Street Health Center, a more commonplace version of the same reminder. The ephemeral floral sculptures Gary Weiss assembles at Ixia, his shop on Market Street. And this short, sharp knife: years after my lover died, years after I'd given his aged cat to a friend living miles away, on a night when I was blindsided by old grief, I encountered that same black cat, wisp of white at his throat, on the steps of my lover's former apartment at Noe and Seventeenth Streets. I have seen too much to seek or require explanation of such mysteries.

*

"All that is human is mine," wrote Terence, the Roman slave and playwright. To the extent that the Castro presents this lesson to a wide audience, it offers public theater at its best: entertaining, didactic, alive; the real-life expression of the writer's imperative (pace Chekhov) to show rather than tell.

On Halloween a few years back I took my Midwestern niece and her husband to the Castro to people-watch. That particular year featured a synchronized swim team dressed in Olympic swimsuits who lay in the middle of Market Street to perform choreographed stunts. As they pointed their toes to the starry night their formation was invaded by two leather men. One pulled a cat-o'-thirty-two-tails from his belt and began flogging his kneeling partner with a delicacy too practiced to be taken seriously; but then I caught the beatific look on the kneeling man's face. What were the stories of his life, that brought him to take pleasure from such public humiliation? I considered diverting my niece's attention elsewhere, then thought better of it.

No such consideration entered my mind when I saw a chain of people dressed in hooded black robes, wearing death masks and carrying scythes, wending their way through the crowd. The drunken, drug-crazed revelers fell back and fell silent. The scene needed no caption.

As the neighborhood grows more gentrified, we hear more loudly the objections to the street people and the public sex. Well, the street people (lest we forget: the children of paradise) we will always have with us. As for public sex, its practitioners could use (in addition to a life) some lessons in the responsibilities attached to participation in the social contract—in exchange for the benefits of living in community, a citizen agrees to give up the most extreme of his or her particular demands and desires. But such civilizing might require the taming of a place where the abnormal sets the standard, where the outrageous is the norm.

That the street demonstrations and occasional sleaze conflict with the neighborhood's increasing investment in bourgeois living is the charming sort of sleight of hand in which fate specializes. A healthy society needs such places, which function as a community's court jester—for a few blocks anyone may shun convention and test the limits of tolerance, sometimes to good ends. There are more baby carriages on the Castro's sidewalks these days, and this is a cheerful sight; but the neighborhood is and ought to remain a place where on a sunny day a courageous man can take off his shirt to reveal his intravenous port.

*

The story of the Castro may be seen as a narrative which represents the evolution of community among gays and lesbians from the darkness and isolation of the closet, through living openly in the material world, to the building of a community illuminated by this basic principle—men *and* women taking care of our own. I doubt if the people involved gave much thought to such a high-falutin goal as creating community. Instead they saw people who needed care, and they set about figuring out how to provide it.

But community manifests itself in particular acts done in particular places for particular people. It is composed of each person acting out of virtue, through which action virtue ceases to be a noble ideal and becomes something as tangible as the Richard Cohen Residence for Homeless with AIDS, or Continuum Services, or the Stop AIDS Project, or Community United Against Violence.

It's too soon to predict whether the gay and lesbian civil rights movement or the gay neighborhoods to which it has given birth will succeed in establishing enduring communities, but the Castro offers plenty of encouraging signs: the rise of lesbians to genuinely egalitarian status; the establishment of philanthropic initiative among our middle class; the movement to establish a neighborhood community center; the dozens of community groups, supported with community willpower and funds, working to enhance and pass on the lessons we have acquired at such great cost.

If popular culture spreads outward from the ghettoes, I want to believe that what is spreading from the Castro is an honest acknowledgment of death and the grief that accompanies it, their necessary place in our lives, and the role of community in preserving and passing on those lessons. This is one definition of community: a means through which people use love to transform suffering and pain into wisdom.

*

I'm back visiting the hamlet where I grew up, eavesdropping from an adjoining room on an elderly friend's bridge club's discussion of gay rights. When one of the women objects to "special rights," another declares that her own son died of AIDS, some years after he moved to the Castro to be cared for by an extended family of gay and straight brothers and sisters. Her brave response moves me to tears. In her speaking up in this place far removed from any city, I understand: change happens, and the men and women of the Castro have been among its agents.

Safe(r) Sex
(1992)

For the Christmas holidays following my lover's death, I returned
to my childhood home. There my mother had bravely placed his
photograph and memorial announcement in a prominent spot,
where everyone might see it and its request for donations to AIDS
charities. At the same time, no one in the family asked after the
story of his death or how I was doing or expressed sympathy. The
contradiction hung over Christmas like emotional smog. My family wanted to be supportive but couldn't bring themselves to break
the silence surrounding so many taboos: my love for men, AIDS,
death. Sunk in grief, I waited for them to speak.

Until three A.M. on the night before I was to return to San
Francisco, one of those white nights between Christmas and New
Year's when several of my nephews, all in their twenties, were sitting around the kitchen table putting a larger dent in the holiday
liquor supply than their parents, my older brothers and sisters,
might have liked. I'd tried twice to go to bed, only to be kept awake
by the knowledge that only the living can do justice to the memory
of the dead. To acquiesce in silence would be to deny and so to
betray their memories, their lives, their loves.

I returned to the kitchen a third time. I opened my mouth: nothing. I hovered at the edge of the conversation, a tongue-tied Ghost

of Christmas Yet to Come, until my next-oldest sister, who'd been keeping company with the next generation, asked bluntly, "What's on *your* mind?"

Her question gave me courage, or at least put me on the spot, and I answered in a breathless torrent of words: "I'm filled with bitterness and rage that no one will acknowledge that my companion was my lover and that he died of AIDS, and I'm here to give the first annual AIDS prevention speech."

Silence. But: rapt attention.

The extent of my hip, college-educated nephews' curiosity turned out to be exceeded only by the magnitude of their ignorance. Their questions ranged from the ludicrous to the touchingly explicit. One understood HIV as more or less omnipresent, like common cold viruses, but precipitated from thin air by the heat of sex. My older sister insisted that she knew a woman who had contracted the virus from sitting in a hot tub with an infected man.

As we talked, I wondered if I was the first person from the preceding generation to speak with my nephews about sex without passing judgment—the first to offer them information with no strings attached. This was far deeper water than I had anticipated, but once off the diving board I had no choice but to swim. If I'd thought before speaking, it would have been to hope that I could talk about HIV without discussing, well, *details*. My nephews were too starved for *details* to allow that. "What about kissing?" one asked.

"I kissed an HIV-positive man for more than three years and I still test negative," I said.

"What about when you're going at it with a girl and she gets all juicy and you get that on your fingers?" another asked, and the question implied its own abyss.

"If you're ignorant of your partner's history, and you have reason to believe she or he may be at risk, you might consider latex gloves." A collective grimace. I fixed my eyes on some imaginary point above and beyond my nephews' heads. "They're not so bad. My lover and I had great, messy sex. Often."

"You're blushing." This from my helpful sister.

"These were our rules." Was I saying this? To my nephews? "We always used condoms. He never came inside me. I never came inside him."

"But wasn't that dangerous?" one asked.

"Life is dangerous!" I cried. "Driving a car is riskier than having safe sex, and you never give driving a second thought. What you do is educate yourself about the risks and then act to minimize them. Have as many partners as you can be careful and considerate with, if that's what you want. Careful *and* considerate. But if nothing else, be careful. If you do needle drugs—"

"Oh, no, we'd never be that stupid," they chorused.

"I'm glad to hear it, but I'm not asking if you'd be that stupid. That's a different talk. I'm telling you how to take care of yourselves."

The next day I rode to the airport with one of my brothers. When I told him I'd delivered the first annual AIDS prevention speech to his sons, he was pleased. Then he told me that, as part of his job, he delivered AIDS awareness talks to his fellow employees. *So why haven't you delivered one to your kids?* I thought, but I said nothing, even though my own experience taught me the answer. Once again my courage evaporated in the face of the great silence.

My nephews' questions might have been naïve, but I left for San Francisco wondering why I had kept silent for so long among my family. I was the one who had known about HIV for years, after all. I had watched friends and a lover grow sick and die, and yet I had said nothing on my visits among those who have no ready access to information, for whom my speaking might make the greatest difference. Why had I found it so hard to act among my family—to speak out among people whom I love?

An easy explanation leapt to mind, one that let me off the hook. It was because these were matters of the heart. The emotions that brought me to care in the first place stifled my tongue.

Well, partly. But I was also trying to preserve my most cherished illusion—that of mind over matter, reason over intuition, choice over fate. To address sex and death at the same time, as talking about HIV required, meant giving up that illusion.

Thinking about these events on the plane, I came to understand that something more than HIV education was behind my Christmas speech to my middle-American nephews. I wanted them to understand HIV and its means of transmission, but I also wanted to get them thinking about the cheerful diversity of sexuality and the miraculously infinite ways of being in the world. I wanted to get them thinking about the enormity of the gap between the tidy, manageable world we pretend to and advertise and the great, sprawling, mysterious world in which we really live. I hoped to bring them to make their own connections between even the most casual sex and some kind of love: caring enough for one's partner and oneself to establish and respect limits.

And I understood that I'd spoken out for my own well-being as much as for theirs. I needed to free myself of lies. I needed truth, which, I was discovering, was not to be accomplished in any single gesture but had to be lived out day by day, act by act.

I returned for the following Christmas, but this time my nephews drove me to the airport. I seized the chance to deliver the second annual AIDS prevention speech, but what was important this time was less the passing on of information than the conversation that followed. During the hour-plus drive, we talked about genealogy, family history, their father's divorce—how it affected their lives, why he had found it so difficult to talk to them and they to him. I cautioned them against holding the previous generation to unrealistic standards. "Love is about forgiveness," I said—an acknowledgment that the beloved is human and fallible, and a decision to love him or her despite or maybe because of that knowledge.

As we talked, I realized that because I'd spoken out—because I took a risk, because I made myself vulnerable—they'd rewarded me with their trust. I had become for them another, different kind of father: a comrade and repository of family history; a bridge between them and him.

My brother had given his children love of a duration and depth I could only admire and learn from, but my own love had its necessary place. I was younger; I hadn't the inevitable and necessary burden of being father; I could say things to his children that he might never find his way to saying. In this way maybe all of us—grandparents, aunts, uncles, cousins, lovers, parents, friends—could find our ways to our particular roles in defining what family is about. Brought together by a chance alignment of stars, histories, and genes, we could act to build families based on love.

City of Innocence and Plague
(2007)

. . . let history lie
and lie light as the ashes
surrendered to the air off Golden Gate Bridge
—Andrew Jaicks, "City of Innocence and Plague"

I never knew a city before San Francisco. At seventeen years old, not knowing how to take a bus or use a pay telephone or order from a menu, clutching a scholarship underwritten by a bourbon distiller, I came directly from the Kentucky hills to the Bay Area. I was drawn by the hippies whose images and stories had made their ways into my childhood. I was drawn by the hope that someone would help me avoid the war in Vietnam. I was drawn by the photographs in the Stanford University catalogue of hunky guys in Speedos lounging under the palm trees by Lake Lagunita, and by the temptations of a culture where people—men—so effortlessly inhabited their beautiful flesh. It was 1971, a peculiar moment of transition when the most powerful empire in history was in the midst of being shown the fallibility and impermanence of all human creations, especially empires. The nation was on the verge of anarchy. My father kept a loaded handgun in his nightstand to shoot the rioters when, not if, they rampaged out of the city into our tiny, remote village.

By the time I arrived, the hippies had fled the Haight and I had to engineer a conscientious objectorship on my own but, even so, I was in California, a word that still carries a frisson of promise and magic. I saw the place in the waning moments of its glory, before the onslaught of real estate madness. Every drive from Palo Alto to the beach was a mystical journey, climbing mountains higher than I had ever seen on a road more crooked than any I had driven to enter a forest taller and deeper than any I'd known—and then, at the road's end, the cold and restless Pacific, free for all, where on a crowded day I might encounter four or five people on a vast beach strewn with exotica, kelp and driftwood and anemones and starfish, and from which I caught a split-second glimpse of a whale hurling its surreally vast self completely out of the water, to fall back with a *thwack!* audible above the crashing surf.

Then the draft ended and the young white men who then as now had ready access to the reins of power went back to the business of making money, lots of money. The sixties died on the morning in 1973 when Secretary of Defense Melvin Laird stood before banks of cameras and microphones and announced the end of the lottery for compulsory military service. And so ended the nation's most extraordinary experiment in democracy, real democracy, where the sons of the privileged were almost as likely to be called upon to defend their privilege as the sons of the poor.

Thirty years and more pass and San Francisco is gussified and prettified and many of those who made it what it is are dead and many of those who remain are struggling to afford to live here. Real estate and microchips dominate every conversation. Almost no one smokes tobacco. People use drugs not for illusions of revelation but for illusions of power—we have transitioned from marijuana to meth. In these dark days of the Republic anyone who's not depressed or angry isn't paying attention, but antidepressants stand in nicely for the soma of Huxley's *Brave New World*. The future is now. We have dug our graves and we lie in them, complacent.

All the dead are present to me in these streets. I find the possibility and promise of progress not in the City's perennial protests against the American empire's latest adventures in imperialism but in the stories of the men and women who cared for our own at a time when many of those paid to do the job shirked their task. At the edge of a nation hellbent on making money we were a throwback in history, a microcosm of medieval London in the midst of the plague. Scorned by our president, vilified by our ministers and priests, uncertain of the threat to our own health, men and women walked into rooms and cared for the dying and the dead. Much has been written of those times but no one has yet captured their extraordinary alembic, the transformation of anger into love, the cool gray city of love.

I confess I do not believe in time. I confess I do not believe in death.

*

As much as any other quality, self-obsession enables San Francisco to consider itself in the league of larger, more powerful cities. New York City, Mexico City, Los Angeles, San Francisco—these are the North American cities where often as not dinner table conversation centers not on politics or culture but on the city itself. This is different from say, Louisville or Tucson, to name smaller cities I happen to know intimately. Residents of those cities think of themselves first as fathers, mothers, children, rich men, poor men, beggarmen, thieves; only later, much later do they consider place as part of their identities—perhaps because many of them live where they were born and raised and so take their place for granted. Residents of New York City, Mexico City, Los Angeles, San Francisco count being a New Yorker, a *Chilango*, an Angeleno, a San Franciscan high, even chief, among their ways of establishing a sense of who they are—perhaps because more often than not they came from someplace else. "You don't have a home until you leave it," writes James Baldwin in *Giovanni's Room*, "and then, when you have left it, you can never go back."

I know this because I came from someplace else and then I left. I lived in San Francisco for much of my adult life and expected that I would call it home until that day when, to use the vernacular of my childhood, I passed on to that greater City on a Hill. In those days when I traveled and told people I was a San Franciscan they'd get this dreamy look. "Oh, I've always wanted to live in San Francisco," they'd say. Then dissatisfaction and a lost apartment took me to New York, an easier city in so many ways. Opportunities knocked, doors opened. During those years when I told people I was a New Yorker they'd get jazzed. "That must be really exciting," they'd say. These days when I tell strangers I live in Tucson, Arizona, there's a rich pause as they search to say something affirming or at least polite. Invariably they resort to "Gee, it's really hot there, isn't it?"

What surprised me, a therapy survivor: how much I had invested my sense of self in my interrogator's response. I *wanted* that dreamy look, that jazzed response; I wanted to be envied on the basis of the place where I'd chosen to hang my hat.

I have lived away from San Francisco for ten years, a figure that astonishes me even as I write it. I have never gone more than a few months without returning, often for long visits, but despite the glamor attached to the phrase "divides his time between," the fact is that only the rarest and biggest of souls can be a responsible citizen of more than one place. Being a good citizen takes time and there's only so much time. It requires living with a place through its troubles as well as its glories. In Tucson that means staying through the summers but I don't stay through the summers. I flee the brutal desert heat for the cool gray city of love.

Long and happy experience has taught me that interesting, engaged people are to be found all over the world, from Kentucky to San Francisco to New York, though the cost of living in the latter cities is slowly draining them of all but the fortunate and the money-grubbers. All the same, I am finding it hard to lay claim to Tucson—in the words of one visitor, "Dusty, sprawling, scrappy, enchanting Tucson"—in the way that I once claimed the Knobs of Kentucky, or the hills of San Francisco, or the streets of New York.

*

Some years ago I wrote, "Places shape people rather than the other way around." With moderation born of experience I amend that sentence to read, "Places shape people *as well as* the other way around." The steep hills divide the city into neighborhoods isolated from one another so that each develops its peculiar character. The vast supply of redwood that lay within a stone's throw, the relative paucity of brick and stone, and construction techniques arising from technological innovations contributed toward ensuring a new and different kind of city from those of the East and of Europe. After the invention of the balloon frame house and the coping saw, could drag queens be far behind? From permanence to transience, from stone and brick to insubstantial wood, from reality to illusion. Boston sits ponderous on the earth; San Francisco is poised to rise with its famously steep hills into its airy-fairy fogs.

The city is the synecdoche of the West, the expression in gingerbread-bedecked wood of people who came here because they wanted to leave reality behind to create and inhabit a myth. Inspect the backside of a Boston Victorian, and you find patterned brick and filigreed stone that complement the building's public face. Inspect the backside of a San Francisco Victorian and you find a plain wooden box—the frills and gewgaws are so much makeup, applied to a stage-set city. Did gay people—of necessity students of deception—settle in here because it is a fantasy city? Or has it become a fantasy city because we settled here? Which came first, the chicken or the egg, the fantasy city or the drag and leather queens and dykes who call it home?

San Francisco is vain to the point of narcississm; like all narcissists, it exists to be loved and has only a dim idea of what it means to give love back. So much about the city is better now—why complain? In a little more than a decade the vile Embarcadero Freeway is gone, to be replaced by a farmer's market. The new baseball stadium has made South of Market a happy, civilized logjam. Light rail reaches parts of the city that have never seen it. There are new palaces for art and performance—each a bit sterile for my taste but handsome all the same.

But few artists and performers can afford to live in a city that worships the grueling, transformative, transcendent process of art less than the social scene that accompanies it once it is finished, dead, pinned to the wall or the page. I write this not as complaint but as observation—better a new de Young Museum than a new freeway—but San Francisco is not as interesting a city as when I first set foot in it. Money, which has so much power to corrupt, has done its work, and then there are all those fine people dead from the plague. The young bohemians who once congregated in the Haight, then the Mission have scattered to the fringes or to smaller, cheaper cities.

San Francisco will always be more interesting than Dallas or Columbus—the San Andreas Fault will see to that—but I find it sad to watch from afar as it sells its haecceity, its thisness, its soul. Once people came here because they wanted to live on the edge, the literal, precarious, teetering edge of the West. Now, driving across the Bay Bridge, returning from one of my absences, I glanced at the jumble of skyscrapers and thought helplessly, *Manhattan*, and though the comparison is hardly original I was troubled by the spontaneity with which it came to mind.

At the same time, the struggle of those to make and keep San Francisco edgy is richer because the more challenging, and in any case, if the train is speeding toward the broken trestle, the more interesting seat is on board. For is this not the place where we were meant to live: in the present, on the cusp, in the corporeal flesh, here and now? San Franciscans' fatal flaw is to misunderstand the object of our adoration. We style it the City—not even New Yorkers are so fixed on the habit—but in fact it is only another of the infinite names of God, a word I use to name this present moment, this here and now.

That is what the City is losing—its delight in living on the edge of the Western world, its civic investment in the here and now. Perhaps only the San Andreas Fault can bring it back.

From the Depths:
Oscar Wilde's De Profundis in Its Second Century
(2009)

Among our immortal dead perhaps only Jesus fell faster and farther: in May 1895 Oscar Wilde's comedy *The Importance of Being Earnest* opened to rave reviews and sold-out houses; by September the play had been closed and he was in prison, after three humiliating trials which left him bankrupt and in debt to the vindictive father of his lover Lord Alfred Douglas ("Bosie"). Nearing the end of his two-year sentence for "acts of gross indecency," Wilde wrote *De Profundis* as a letter to Bosie, sending it shortly after his release, though Bosie claimed never to have received it. A bowdlerized edition was posthumously published in 1905; the full text did not see print until 1962.

Born to prosperity in Ireland in 1854, raised in the wake of the great potato famine, Wilde grew up amid a foment of rebellion and mysticism—the most reasonable responses to unreasonable suffering. His life and art are a movement from the former to the latter—from the elegant libertinism of the fiction, plays, and poetry to the mystic's search for meaning and redemption in *De Profundis*.

In part because of the conditions of its composition, *De Profundis* is frankly a mess. Wilde was not allowed pen and paper until

well into the second year of his sentence; once granted these priv-
ileges, he was not allowed to retain or review each day's work,
meaning that in writing he had to rely on memory for organization and continuity. Those looking to read Wilde's most polished
material are better served by *The Picture of Dorian Gray*, the plays,
or the profound and touching *Ballad of Reading Gaol*.

The easy advice would be to read only the letter's eloquent later
pages, skipping the finger-pointing and breast-beating of its first
half. But that would be to miss the great pageant of the work—the
pilgrim's progress from empiricist to mystic, the boulevardier of
the cities of the plain to the prophet of the mountains, the lesser
to the greater man. The lesser man must berate and blame; the
greater man will be an artist in spite of his flaws—it is his vocation
and his destiny. *De Profundis* charts Wilde's journey—in real time,
so to speak, given the circumstances under which it was written.

The defining quality of genius—as distinguished from ambi-
tion, which is commonplace, and talent, which is unusual but in-
sufficient—may lie in its holder's capacity to fashion a scrim onto
which we can project and so perceive the secret, unacknowledged
aspects of our own characters. Wilde was an undisputed master
of such fabrications, but the horrors of Reading Gaol tore away
the scrim. Every lover of beauty must read these pages, because
of their revelation of the desires and illusions that we project onto
their author and for their portrayal of the conflicts of the soul
behind the scrim.

*

Long before his imprisonment, Wilde had spoken to gay French
novelist André Gide of his intention to present the life of Jesus,
including the Crucifixion, as the ultimate work of art and thus Jesus as the avatar of aestheticism, the philosophy—for which Wilde
had become the world-famous proponent—that art need serve no
moral or practical purpose. But he did not or could not undertake
the task until after he had endured his own crucifixion—until he
became or made of himself a martyr.

As every artist knows or learns, art is about process more than product. The book or painting or performance is the fruit of what philosopher Jacques Maritain called "the habit of art," but—to extend the metaphor—the life itself is the tree: that which bears the fruit. In Wilde's Church of Beauty the finished products are merely the fruits of a life that is in and of itself the greatest work of art. In *De Profundis* he offers Jesus's life as the most perfect example: "[Christ] is just like a work of art," he writes. "He does not really teach one anything but by being brought to his presence one becomes something."

"What the artist is looking for is the mode of existence in which soul and body are one and indivisible," Wilde writes. This achievement of nonduality, as Buddhism would have it, or union with Beauty, as Plato would have it, or union with God in Jewish, Christian, or Sufi terminology is the heart of the mystic's enterprise, whatever the source tradition. For Wilde, art was the means to that end: "Truth in art is the unity of a thing with itself . . . the secret of life is suffering." The first half of the statement has its roots in Plato, the second in the Passion Play of Jesus's life and death.

*

As a vehicle for this mode of living Wilde imagines a new, apophatic church: "Religion does not help me," he writes.

> The faith that others give to what is unseen, I give to what one can touch, and look at. . . . I would like to found an order for those who *cannot* believe . . . agnosticism must have its ritual no less than faith. It has sown its martyrs, it should reap its saints, and praise God daily for having hidden himself from man.

In these eloquent later pages Wilde speaks with the voice of the prophet and mystic whom prison has taught to embrace suffering as wisdom's necessary condition—"the price of the ticket," in James Baldwin's apt rendering. "Clergymen and people who use phrases without wisdom sometimes talk of suffering as a mystery," Wilde writes. "It is really a revelation. . . whatever happens to one-self happens to another"—an inverted restatement of Matthew 25:40, "inasmuch as you did it to one of the least of these My brethren, you did it to Me."

But a worm dwells at the heart of the gorgeous prose. Biog-rapher Richard Ellmann writes that in *De Profundis*, Wilde "en-visaged [an] essay to deal with . . . Christ as the supreme artist and Wilde as his prophet." But even in these later pages Wilde is no one's prophet but his own. His intense self-awareness—the price of the ticket of being born to unconventional desires—pre-vents him from attaining Jesus's characteristic simplicity except in glimpses. Wilde was born and raised in Catholic Ireland, yes, but of Protestant, Anglo-Irish parents, and though he romanticized the Roman church of "saints and sinners," in fact he owed his suc-cess to the institutions and society of Anglican England and was as committed as any good Protestant to the preeminence of indi-vidual achievement. In *De Profundis* he invokes Jesus's suffering while never touching upon the Resurrection and its attendant promise of union with God—or, as Plato would have it, Beauty.

The omission provides insight into Wilde's divided sensibilities: as an Irish-born mystic, martyr, and megalomaniac he embraces Jesus's story, with its many parallels with his own life (deserted by friends as Jesus was deserted by his disciples; rejecting opportu-nities to flee England as Jesus chose to remain in the Garden of Gethsemane). The "four prose poems" of the Gospels from which Wilde drew his inspiration inextricably couple the martyred and the risen Jesus. Their conflation is precisely the work of art Wilde invokes when he writes, "An idea is of no value until it is become incarnate and made an image." Jesus's Crucifixion and Resurrec-tion incarnate, in a simple, unforgettable story and in indelible images, the ideas at the heart of Wilde's aestheticism and of the Platonic philosophy on which it drew.

But as a post-Enlightenment empiricist Wilde cannot bring himself even to mention the risen Jesus, whose Resurrection is the logical, inevitable culmination of the story—the fruit of the tree, the work of art to which the life has pointed and led. The schizophrenic structure of *De Profundis* correlates this intellectual/spiritual divide: In the opening pages Wilde the empiricist places Bosie on trial, seeking a logical sequence of events that might explain Wilde's own fall from grace and in the process justify his behavior. In the later pages Wilde the mystic arrives at the understanding of his fall as a combination of the ineluctable workings of destiny and what essayist Phillip Lopate wryly calls "the catastrophe of character." At various points in the essay's opening pages Wilde writes, "I blame myself," "I ceased to be lord over myself," and (to Bosie) "You were absolutely responsible." In the later pages he makes an about-face to arrive at the place where he can observe, "The gods are strange. They bring us to ruin through what in us is good, gentle, human, loving."

The notion that we are always and everywhere in control of our destinies is a peculiarly Western affliction, given lie by the existence of people whose innate desires set us on unconventional paths. Together with the transcripts of Wilde's trials, *De Profundis* remains not just fascinating but necessary reading because it chronicles the education of a great artist out of that particular myth, in the process offering an unsettling exploration of the conflict between reason's absolute need to know and the necessarily unknowable recesses of the heart.

*

I take as self-evident that the horrors of prison broke Wilde's spirit and that as a result he turned to philosophy and religion, but I find this cause not for dismissal of the work but an imperative for its reading. When Nietzsche tells us that Christianity is Platonism for the masses, he points up not its weakness but the source of its enduring strength: religion—that peculiar, deeply flawed blend of passion and principle—is our most successful effort at making the comforts of philosophy available to the mass of people in a form that they can comprehend and at least aspire to live by.

Like art itself, the artist "is of his very essence quite useless," Wilde writes, but *De Profundis* offers prima facie refutation of its own logic. As Wilde repeatedly points out, art springs from the imagination, and the most profound acts of imagination require that we rise above our particular circumstances to consider our sufferings as threads in the great tapestry of human sorrow. This is the noblest aspiration and function of philosophy—of religion—of art—of writing: the transformation of suffering into beauty, broadly defined as harmony with the divine order of the universe. "To propose to be a better man is a piece of unscientific cant," Wilde writes. "To have become a deeper man is the privilege of those who have suffered. And such I think I have become." Considered in this light, philosophy, religion, art, writing may be our most potent evolutionary tools.

*

Wilde writes that prison has been the ruin of his career, though with the hindsight of a century the opposite seems true regarding his longer-term reputation. Had he never met Bosie, Wilde would surely have found a different, equally powerful catalyst for martyrdom; had he never endured prison we would still perform his plays and of his prose read at least *Dorian Gray*. But the notoriety of the trials and his imprisonment elevated his life from the merely brilliant to something closer to the immortality—in religious terms, sainthood—to which he aspired. Martyrdom is so much more interesting than ordinary mortality, and Wilde was a passionate devotee of all that is interesting. After he had conquered the pinnacle of material success, what remained to explore but the topography of descent? The very thesis of *De Profundis* is that his time in prison has been a great gift, without which he could never have learned the lessons he is setting forth.

Early in *De Profundis* Wilde writes that he must learn again "how to be cheerful and happy," a goal he can reach only by finding beauty in his terrible fate. But once freed, despite his eloquently argued principles, he returned to his old ways in different streets.

He lived, in fact, Jesus's Passion without its payoff. He seems to have found happiness only in glimpses, partly because life denied him the time—he died three and a half years later, of uncertain causes surely provoked or worsened in prison—but partly because, though he took Jesus as his model, his humility was imposed upon rather than organic to his character. He never embraced the ultimate humility—the submission of reason to the manifestly unreasonable story of the Resurrection.

Like Milton's Satan—the most likeable character in *Paradise Lost*—Wilde preferred noble rebellion to humble submission, at least until his deathbed. There he completed the mystical journey by converting to Roman Catholicism, a transition that allowed him to live in the empiricist's celebration of individual genius but die in the communitarian embrace of Mother Church.

In life as in theater, timing is all.

*

These days Wilde is often identified as a "gay writer," but I wonder whether he would have welcomed the label. Rather than as a gay writer I think of him as an outsider of the type elaborated by philosopher Colin Wilson, "a man who cannot live in the comfortable, insulated world of the bourgeois. . . . It is not simply the need to cock a snook at respectability that provokes him; it is a distressing sense that *truth must be told at all costs*." Late in *De Profundis*, though writing of Hamlet, Wilde is clearly describing himself: "a dreamer . . . a poet . . . asked . . . to grapple with life in its practical realization, of which he knows nothing, not with life in its ideal essence, of which he knows so much." Wilde was placed in the dock as much for his flamboyant effeminacy as for what he did in bed; for his refusal to hide as much as for what he was hiding. The "order" he proposes to found is not a great edifice of pomp and regulations but something humbler: an order of and for outcasts whose saint is a criminal; an order that Jesus ("counted among the transgressors," Luke 22:37) might have founded; an order for me and—maybe—for you.

"You came to me to learn the pleasure of life and the pleasure of art," Wilde concludes *De Profundis*, addressing us, his future readers, more than Bosie. "Perhaps I am chosen to teach you
something more wonderful—the meaning of sorrow and its beauty." If that strikes our postmodern, pleasure-principled ears as too
self-consciously penitential, consider the following from Emily
Dickinson, a near-contemporary and another student of suffering:

> I like a look of Agony,
> Because I know it's true—
> Men do not sham Convulsion,
> Nor simulate, a Throe—

"Sorrow is the ultimate type in both life and art," Wilde writes, a
statement that evokes particular poignance for its proximity to *The
Importance of Being Earnest*, one of our most sparkling comedies and
his last work prior to *De Profundis*. "Behind joy and laughter there
may be a temperament, coarse, hard, and callous. But behind sorrow there is always sorrow. Pain, unlike pleasure, wears no mask."
After the degradations of prison, become as intimate with suffering as with any lover, Wilde can write of Jesus, "In a manner not
yet understood of the world he regarded sin and suffering as being
in themselves beautiful and holy things and modes of perfection."
   Far from useless, this lesson may be the most important life can
teach: the ripping away of the veil of maya, as Hinduism would
have it, to reveal the fundamental unity of all creation, including pleasure and pain, joy and suffering. It lies at the heart of all
the great wisdom traditions, but Wilde—perhaps, after Jesus, our
greatest aphorist—sums it up most succinctly and eloquently:
"The past, the present, and the future are but one moment in the
sight of God . . . time and space, succession and extension are
merely accidental conditions of thought."
   "Love is fed by the imagination," Wilde writes, "by which we
become wiser than we know, better than we feel, nobler than we
are." Having lived in San Francisco in the first decades of the
AIDS pandemic I cannot help finding in Wilde's suffering and

in *De Profundis* a prefiguring and a primer for that later, vaster trauma. In both tragedies—one particular, one general—one may find evidence of the cruel senselessness of life or, not in the pandemic but in the gay community's response to it, the beauty which Wilde, taking his cue from Jesus, understood as the perfection toward which we must progress.

Part III

Power and Obedience:
Restoring Pacifism to American Politics
(2014)

I

We were four brothers who came of age in lockstep with the escalating war in Vietnam.

In 1964, in keeping with an ancient tradition in which, seeking social and economic advancement, men from blue-collar backgrounds risk our lives to fight the wars of the rich, my oldest brother enlisted in the US Air Force. In his case the gamble almost failed—in 1966 he nearly died in a covert operation carried out somewhere near the Laos/North Vietnam border, the details of which the US Air Force never allowed him to reveal since at the time Americans were not officially on the Laos/North Vietnam border. My second brother received deferments that carried him through the war years. Following the eldest's example, my third brother joined the US Marines in 1971, spending his years of service in domestic and international assignments. In that same year, on my eighteenth birthday, I filed with the Nelson County, Kentucky, Selective Service board as a conscientious objector (CO).

Not long before these events, in response to outrage over a system that provided escape routes for the rich (President George W. Bush) or the clever (President Bill Clinton), Congress had largely eliminated deferments and exemptions, inaugurating a lottery in their stead. Men's eligibility was determined by a number, assigned by random selection based on birthdate. Of men born in 1952, those with numbers lower than 095 had been called up.

The lottery for men born, like me, in 1953 was conducted February 2, 1972, at nine A.M. Eastern time. The men of my dorm rose at six A.M. to watch it broadcast. Trusting to the gods, I stayed abed, to be awakened by whoops from those who had received high numbers and by the audible hush outside my door. My number was 009, the lowest in my dorm.

The following summer, though many of us were still shy of the induction age of nineteen, men from my county were bused to the Louisville VA hospital for medical examinations. What my high school debate research taught in the abstract, that day illustrated in fact: the war was being fought by poor urban blacks and poor rural whites. The bus was filled with boys—men—like me, some of them my grade school classmates, with this exception: their education had stopped at high school. Most assumed they would be sent to Vietnam, a prospect they viewed with unbridled enthusiasm.

Two weeks later I was classified 1-A, eligible for service. My local draft board denied my written application, now almost a year old, for a CO; I filed an appeal. I submitted the paperwork in person. The draft board secretary studied it carefully. She knew me, of course; she'd seen my picture in the local paper—state champion extemporaneous speaker, president of the state student senate, the sort of boy about whom the locals said, "That boy will be governor someday." "Are you sure you want to do this," she said—a statement, not a question. "Yes, ma'am," I answered. With a country woman's understanding of the ways of the world, she said, "Forget about a career in politics," and of course she was right.

On the afternoon of the hearing, held in September 1972, I told my mother I was going on a date and asked her to cut my hair. I borrowed the car and picked up two high school teachers who had agreed to serve as character witnesses.

My northern California counseling had not prepared me for the board's first question: "What the hell is a son of P. D. Johnson doing here?" The hearing lasted two hours, during which I gave the rhetorical performance of my young life.

Afterward, in anticipation of an appeal, I was required to record my version of the evening. I was covering page after page when the secretary emerged from the hearing room. I asked when I could learn the outcome and was told that I'd receive a letter "in a week or two." The board met monthly. "That means they'll make a decision tonight," I said. I was an eighteen-year-old country boy defying convention and my elders. I was about to leave for my university's study-abroad program in France, an impossible prospect for someone from my background—in my ancestors' long history on this continent, not one had traveled abroad, except, of course, as a soldier—but already I had decided that if I did not receive my CO, I would not return. With assertiveness born of terror and conviction I said, "I'll wait until they make a decision." She returned to the hearing room. Some fifteen minutes later she emerged. "You can phone tomorrow and find out," she said. I returned to scribbling. "If I can phone tomorrow, then they're making a decision tonight." She returned to the committee room, to emerge after another fifteen minutes. "You got it," she said. I stopped writing in midsentence, handed her the papers, and left.

Back home, I raided my parents' liquor cabinet to pour a drink for my teachers. The phone rang—it was my mother calling to ask someone to turn off the heat under the pot roast. "I thought you were on a date," she said. "I had my CO hearing," I said. "I got it." A moment of pregnant silence. In a voice devoid of inflection she said, "Good." The subject was never mentioned again. Years later she gave me a box containing, she said, all my correspondence. My letter announcing my decision to apply for a CO, which above all others I longed to read, was missing.

I believe mine to be the only CO my draft board granted in its history. I owe that decision to the county's wounded and dead. Nearly forty years later a local filmmaker would claim that on a per capita basis my home county—1970 population: 23,477—lost more men in Vietnam than any other county in America. Seven Nelson Countians died in one especially brutal day in 1969, an event memorialized in granite on the courthouse square. By the time of that September evening in 1972 my draft board, like the country, was sick of the war. Its decision, rendered in the heartland of patriotism, was a measure of how sick.

As of this writing 4,359 American soldiers, men and women, have died in Iraq and another 954 in Afghanistan, for a total of 5,313 dead. 30,182 are recorded as wounded in Iraq alone, a figure that does not include those who return home too traumatized to function, some of whom will become tomorrow's drug abusers and homeless. To date the wars have cost over $1 trillion. For the same expenditure, assuming the pre-war per capita annual income of $700 (Iraq) or $500 (Afghanistan), the United States could have supported every Iraqi or Afghani for more than twenty years. Instead conservative estimates count well over 100,000 Iraqi civilians dead, the Iraq economy is in ruins, and the influence of the Taliban and Al-Qaeda arguably stronger than when the wars began.

II

Men will seek beauty, whether in life or in death.
—Krishna to Arjuna on the battlefield of
Kurukṣetra, *Bhagavad-Gita*

Almost forty years have passed and I am standing outside the Titan Missile Museum, some thirty miles south of Tucson, Arizona, beneath the terraced tailings of an open-pit copper mine. The tailings are barren even of cactus, but teddy-bear cholla and mesquite and creosote struggle through the tawny grit at the parking lot's edge. A vast American flag flutters and snaps against the deep cloudless blue of a December desert sky.

The museum is housed in a warehouse of blue corrugated steel. Dedication plaques are mounted on slabs of granite. The principal donors ($50,000) are the largest local auto dealer, James Click Jr.; the National Park Association; and Count Ferdinand von Galen, a Transylvanian-esque name that demands taking note. My tour is filled: twenty-five people, twelve Anglo couples and me.

In the early 1960s the United States built Titan Missile sites near the cities of Little Rock, Arkansas, Wichita, Kansas, and Tucson. The eighteen silos surrounding Tucson took twenty-eight months to be completed and declared combat-ready at a cost of $12.8 million each. The officers in charge of each site carried side arms "in the event of an uncooperative crew member." A computer archive housed in the museum lobby includes a film from the period, produced and distributed by the Federal Civil Defense Administration, interspersing staged footage of schoolchildren crawling under desks with a cartoon turtle singing "Duck and cover!" A man's voice intones, "That flash means: Act fast! We must be ready to do the right thing at any time when the atomic bomb explodes." Onscreen, girls in yoked jumpers drop ropes in midskip and head into the gym. A boy in a starched white shirt leaps from his bicycle and buries his head in a gutter ("Johnny knows any shelter is good"). A family in a park hides under their picnic blanket.

Our tour guides are Bob (aquiline nose, thin upper lip, big ears) and George (plank skinny, a dried rosebud for a mouth, big ears).

Both are Air Force Titan II crew veterans. Bob speaks fast, occasionally asking, "Are there any questions?" but not inviting any. George has his name printed in large letters on the bill of his blue hardhat. In the next one and one-half hours he will say two words.

Bob leads us outside to a display of the missile engines, overbuilt versions of the internal combustion engine Henry Ford popularized. Each missile was capable of 5.5 minutes of propelled flight that took it over 200 miles into the air. "Thirty-five thousand gallons in five minutes and nobody's worrying about fuel efficiency," Bob says. From that point it operated on inertia, a metal canister with multiple nuclear warheads in its cone, coasting in a long gentle arc to earth.

The missiles had "point-eight accuracy," which Bob defines as "if they fired one hundred, half would land within eight-tenths of a mile of their targets." He does not say what would have happened with the other half. Accuracy was not the point. According to Bob, the warheads they carried were nine thousand times more powerful than the bomb dropped on Hiroshima. They would have produced a three-mile-wide fireball. Everything and everyone within nineteen miles would have been instantly incinerated. The Strategic Air Command (SAC) named the policy Mutual Assured Destruction, "or MAD," Bob says, "a perfect acronym for what would have happened. It worked great for fifty years."

We descend honeycombed metal stairs into the silo. Stenciled throughout are reminders of the "No Lone Zone" policy: crew members were never allowed to be out of each other's sight. Bob demonstrates the door to the control room—over a foot thick, weighing eight tons. A fellow tourist pulls it forward with one hand. "Hung a half inch above the floor and that's where it still hangs, fifty years later," Bob says. Christmas is coming, his tone is festive. "You know what an elephant is?" We look at him blankly. "Come on, bite. Somebody. Anybody." "What's an elephant," I say. "A mouse designed by nuclear engineers," he says.

The control panels are simple. A few rows of lights labeled in clear sequence, ready, fire, no need to aim—the crew never knew their targets and weren't empowered to change them. To one side, a black Bakelite dial telephone, the same black Bakelite phone that hangs beside the doors of aging apartment buildings. Greenwich Time was kept with a wind-up clock.

In one corner sits the home of the secret codes—a battered two-drawer metal filing cabinet painted a saturated crimson and featuring a dial lock and two small padlocks. Bob runs down the checklist of steps to be performed if the Bakelite phone rang. "Everything by the numbers in SAC," he says, a mantra of his talk. "Once you turned the key you abandoned control of the missile. There were no mulligans."

After the signing of the SALT II treaty SAC turned this site into a museum, removing the missile's cap and laying it out on the ground so the Russians could take pictures from their satellites to verify it had been decommissioned. All other Titan II sites were destroyed and the properties sold. "If you need proof that God has a sense of humor," Bob says, "there's a church sitting atop one site."

From the first I've been bothered by the question *Would he have done it?* If the call had come, the order given, the codes checked out, would this amiable guy-next-door have pushed the button that destroyed civilization? As if in response to my question he barks, not a request but a command. "I need a volunteer!" No one steps forward. We know what's coming. The hesitation is palpable.

With their infallible sense of humor, the gods have placed me closest to the control panel chair. For other visitors to volunteer they would have to step over me. So I sit in the chair—four wheels, military-issue gray Naugahyde patched with duct tape.

The button turns out to be not a button but a small aluminum-alloy key of the type that opens a gym locker. Bob gives rapid instructions containing lots of numbers. "You got that?" "Uh, no," I say. He screws up his face. "You a schoolteacher?" "Well, yes." He sighs. "I knew it. Teachers can give orders but can't take 'em."

I so want to believe this to be true. It would explain so much—why as a kid I liked school, why I filed for a CO, why I became a teacher.

Behind my back one of the other tourists explains: When he gives the signal, count to five and turn the key. I'm staring at the silent bank of lights. Bob crosses to a companion desk. "One-and-two-and-three." He turns a key. "OK, your turn."

And I'm staring at the sleeping panel of lights with their key, well-worn from many turnings. Conscientious objector at eighteen, forty years a pacifist, here's my second chance to say, "I can't do it. I won't do it." We are many feet underground in a tiny windowless space. At my back the eyes of the twelve Anglo couples. Across from me sits Bob, impatient with the schoolteacher who can't take orders.

I turn the key. The lights blink in sequence. I have made a choice, followed orders, played a role, maybe the only role that finally matters in the destruction of civilization.

They had a thirty-day food supply, Bob tells us, and thirty days' worth of recycled air, "or that's what they told us." Later I overhear him tell another tourist, a US Navy veteran, that when the crews serviced the diesel engines used to fire the missiles they dumped the old fuel down the silo, thus contaminating the air supply. "But who would have wanted to get out," he said.

On the drive home, I think how this is where it all began—the age of paranoia, the beginning of the end of life calibrated on assumptions other than the constant, eternal threat and practice of war. The radio tells me that the CEOs of various Wall Street banks, so recently brought by their managements to the brink of collapse and rescued by the government, have declined the president's invitation to meet in Washington. A gutted version of national health care is struggling to pass the Senate. In Copenhagen international leaders squabble over whether nations are capable of slowing climate change. I turned the key.

From the *New York Times*, July 8, 1986: "A Frankfurt court today convicted Ferdinand von Galen, former head of the prestigious West German bank Schroder-Munchmeyer-Hengst, of breach of trust. He was sentenced to three years and nine months in prison for his role in the bank's reaching the verge of collapse."

Count Ferdinand von Galen emerged from prison to immigrate first to California, then Arizona, domestic Paraguay for white-collar criminals. Here he is a land developer, major donor to the

Titan Missile Museum, and supporter of the local Roman Catholic Church, which teaches that God forgives all sins of the genuinely penitent heart.

III

Experience proves that the man who obstructs a war in which his nation is engaged, no matter whether right or wrong, occupies no enviable place in life or history. Better for him, individually, to advocate "war, pestilence, and famine," than to act as obstructionist to a war already begun. . . . The most favorable posthumous history the stay-at-home traitor can hope for is—oblivion.

—Ulysses S. Grant, *Personal Memoirs*

In his eloquent *Memoirs*, Ulysses Grant condemns the "stay-at-home traitor" to "oblivion," but let us consider the fates of Grant's contemporaries, the four brothers of New England's famous James family. The two brothers who fought in the Civil War suffered from what today we call post-traumatic stress syndrome: wounded in battle, Wilky was plagued by ill health and financial difficulties for the rest of his short life; Robertson drifted aimlessly, an alcoholic with a violent temper. Meanwhile Henry and William, the "stay-at-home traitors," achieved enduring international reputations, Henry as a prolific writer, William as the Harvard professor often identified as the founder of modern psychology.

Over a century ago, in our most eloquent argument for pacifism, William James challenged us to find "the moral equivalent of war." His essay "The Moral Equivalent of War" is a masterpiece of rhetoric, a monument of neoclassical prose grounded in the pragmatism he espoused.

"Pacifists ought to enter more deeply into the esthetical and ethical point of view of their opponents," James writes, then heeds his counsel, making an argument for war that Dick Cheney might admire. "The martial virtues . . . are absolute and permanent human goods," he observes, bluntly acknowledging the attraction—indeed, as society is currently structured, the *necessity*—of war. As biologists have demonstrated that the growing tree requires wind and storm to strengthen its trunk, people require challenge to fulfill our greatest destinies—to achieve beauty. "Militarism is the great preserver of our ideals of hardihood, and human life with no use for hardihood would be contemptible," James writes. "I do not believe that peace either ought to be or will be permanent on this globe unless the states, pacifically organized, preserve some of the old elements of army-discipline." The great flaw of pacifism, he observes, is its inability to provide a rival to war as a stimulus for the imagination. "War is the romance of history," he writes, and it will not end until we find or create a story as or more compelling. The pacifist challenge, then, becomes the creation of "the moral equivalent of war"—an ethic and a system that "will speak to men as universally as war does, and yet will be as compatible with their spiritual selves as war has proved itself to be incompatible."

In the course of a decade James reworked the essay, and at different points he proposes different "moral equivalents." In the earlier version, incorporated into his magisterial *Varieties of Religious Experience*, he writes,

> I have often thought that in the old monkish poverty-worship . . . there might be something like that moral equivalent of war for which we are seeking. . . . When one sees the way in which wealth-getting enters as an ideal into the very bone and marrow of our generation, one wonders whether a revival of the belief that poverty is a worthy religious vocation may not be the "transformation of military courage," and the spiritual reform which our time stands most in need of.

> Among English-speaking peoples especially do the praises of poverty need once more to be boldly sung. . . . Think of the strength which personal indifference to poverty would give us if we were devoted to unpopular causes . . . while we lived, we would imperturbably bear witness to the spirit, and our example would help set free our generation.

A decade later, possibly in acknowledgment of the unlikelihood of Americans voluntarily embracing "poverty-worship," James proposed a "conscription of the whole youthful population to form for a certain number of years a part of the army enlisted against *Nature*"—anticipating by a century the opportunities implied in a collective national and international engagement with our environment.

In his campaign President Obama suggested such a service agency, though the idea has since been dropped. And yet, writing from twenty-five years' experience teaching college students, I can report their urgent, ever-intensifying desire to find meaning in their lives beyond market share, their search to be of use to someone other than themselves. Might we teach, as the Buddha and Jesus taught, that the meaning they seek and the power they must obey lie not without but within?

*

Whether James would consider contemporary America as a "state pacifically organized" is open for debate. We have constructed an economy that *requires* the ceaseless preparation for and waging of war, an economy James described with unnerving relevance to our endless wars in the Middle East: "The intensely sharp competitive *preparation* for war by the nations *is the real war*, permanent, unceasing. . . . When the time of development is ripe the war must come, reason or no reason, for the justifications pleaded are invariably fictitious." In James's time that fictitious justification was the sinking of the battleship *Maine* in Havana Harbor; in ours it was "weapons of mass destruction."

The metaphor of war has so thoroughly permeated our public dialogue that we live in it as fish live in water. There are the endless wars in Iraq and Afghanistan, of course, but also the war on poverty, the war on cancer, the war on drugs, the war on terrorism, the cyber war between the United States and China. Former Vice President Cheney asks of President Obama, "Why doesn't he want to admit we're at war?" and the President rises to the bait—both men choosing to overlook that no president of either party has sought the constitutionally required declaration by Congress.

As our economy has become dependent on the manufacture and sale of weapons and as we have made military service the only affordable option for young people from disadvantaged classes seeking to improve their lot, pacifism, once a regular feature of our national political debate, has fallen from unpopularity to invisibility. Even William James proposes an "army" enlisted "against *Nature*," but the most important recent scientific advance may be our renewed acknowledgment of the terrible consequences of being *against* something of which we are an integral part. The great news of the moment is that we have the possibility of enlisting an army not *against* but *for* nature; an army enlisted to heal; a context to practice "the martial virtues" founded in an appeal to our higher selves. People will seek beauty, people *must* seek beauty, whether in taking up the gun or by reclaiming strip-mined Appalachia—the choice is ours.

At the moment when I turned the key, many forces were at work: my very human curiosity to see what would happen next; the murmur of the following tour group, already audible outside the eight-ton door; the pressure of twenty-four pairs of eyes on my back; the exasperation of Bob, our guide, fed up with school-teachers who can't take orders.

But sitting at the Titan II control desk, turning the key, I grasped for a moment the dread and boredom and responsibility of the soldier's life that formed Bob. The point of roping a random tourist into the act was not, finally, to demonstrate the quaint blinking lights of the Titan II console. It was to underscore our complicity in the enterprise, to parcel out the evil implicit in the project.

Now "evil" is a strong word, but to justify its use let us consider World War II, the "good" war. More than 60 million dead, the great majority of them civilians—trauma on a scale that literally defies comprehension. The cities and economies of Europe, the Soviet Union, and Japan laid waste; the introduction of nuclear arms to the world; America (and through us, the world) permanently militarized—this was the *good* war. The liberation of the concentration camps alone might have justified this suffering, but though the Allies knew of the camps they never invoked them as a reason for the war, and in fact America turned away Jewish refugees. Meanwhile churchmen in Germany and England preached the "just" war, arguing that God blessed their atrocities while condemning those of their opponents.

"The war against war is going to be no holiday excursion or camping party," James writes. Such a "war," if we took it seriously, would require courage compared with which the leap into battle is child's play. It would require us, citizens of the empire of this particular historical moment, to grow up, put away childish things, get wiser, believe in and build a better world. It would require us to obey not our baser but our better instincts. It would require us to seek beauty in life instead of death.

You will tell me very reasonably that this is nice in the abstract but hopeless in the execution, and you will be very reasonably correct; but reason unaided is not sufficient to the challenge of extracting us from a mess in which reason is so deeply complicit. That a world without war is an unattainable ideal I do not doubt, but with equal conviction I know that without an ideal as Polaris for our decisions we are lost.

Do immutable flaws in human nature require us to accept war as a given? Or is it possible to imagine and achieve a better world? In the way that we moved from struck flint to light switch, may we move toward a world in which violence is, if not eliminated, at least shorn of its allure? That would require a commitment toward embracing an alternative—a moral equivalent of war. Instead we are engaged in an experiment to prove that military training can dehumanize women as effectively as men.

Maybe the impulse that leads the neighborhood bully to demolish the sand castle must periodically have its way; maybe many small wars relieve the pressure of some atavistic need to destroy what we have built. I am more prepared to accept that logic than the Thomist notion that some wars are just, some violence righteous.

But by definition mercy is a virtue reserved to the powerful. Had we responded to September 11 by spending the $1 trillion devoted to wars in Afghanistan and Iraq on humanitarian projects, abroad and at home, might we now feel more rather than less safe? The brilliance of terrorism is that it lures us off base, goads us into abandoning our finest qualities and ideals—our native generosity and our founding principles, equal justice before law and the right to habeas corpus among them. We undermine our own foundations and so bring to pass our enemies' greatest fantasy: we become like them.

*

We already know what we need to do to diminish war and to heal our broken relationship to the planet. Our wise ones have been delivering the message for thousands of years. Every great wisdom tradition teaches that the true "war"—if it must be so named—is not exterior but interior, not with each other but within our hearts. Our failure is not of technology but of imagination—our incapacity or unwillingness to imagine a world in which we might cultivate "martial" virtues through pacific paths.

A seasoned warrior inadvertently makes my point. On the penultimate page of his Iraq war memoir *One Bullet Away*, Marine Corps Captain Nathaniel Fick writes that he was not proud of what he did: "shooting kids, cowering in terror behind a berm, dropping artillery on people's homes." But he ends his book:

> The good didn't feel as good as the bad felt bad. . . . I hope life improves for the people of Afghanistan and Iraq, but that's not why we did it. We fought for each other.

> I am proud.

Perhaps my pacifism is a remnant of a time when the world held fewer people and the resources to feed and house them seemed inexhaustible. Maybe the Declaration of Independence and the Bill of Rights were convenient covers for greed, and our bourgeois

revolution rooted in our forefathers' obsession with getting rich
unfettered by imperial taxes rather than in their commitment to
liberty and justice. Perhaps we were more jaded but more honest to temper our aspirations for government as an instrument of
human dignity, settling instead for its facilitating the making and
spending of money, in which case a gun is the most useful of tools.
Perhaps, as ancient tribes believed, history is circular and there is
no redemption from our essentially corrupt natures. Perhaps, as
unregulated capitalism requires, nothing is sacred, most particularly the lives of the poor. Every creature and concept carries a
price tag, and beauty is a commodity to be purchased with blood
or money.

But civilization's primary project is to offer our Nathaniel Ficks
ways of seeking beauty. Consider our blocks of blighted urban housing, or deteriorating parks, or understaffed classrooms of inner-
city and rural schools; consider the improvements in prosperity
brought about by basic literacy and preventive medicine programs; consider my students' longing for meaning and purpose,
an outlet for their burning need to use their talents.

Driving past the vacant steel mills of Charleston, West Virginia,
I imagined them equipped with translucent roofs and transformed
into vast greenhouses, employing hundreds in raising hardy winter
greens for delivery to East Coast cities, reducing our petroleum
footprint and providing healthy food and self-respect-generating
employment. In barely two years the American military constructed its Titan Missile sites, each armed with warheads designed to
destroy the planet. What might we achieve if our leaders moti-
vated us not to destroy the Earth but to heal it?

In Between: Fiction Writer as Drag Queen
(2010)

In a novel I recently completed entitled *The Man Who Loved Birds*, a Trappist monk, without understanding what is happening to him, falls in love with a renegade Vietnam vet who grows marijuana. In the course of writing that novel I decided I needed to do some research into drag, since an early draft called for the monk to visit a drag bar and what did I, having never been more than a bemused spectator, know about drag? So I called up my first cousin once removed and flew him to San Francisco to dress me for Halloween.

Now, my first cousin once removed is a Memphis drag queen who moonlights doing makeup on the corpses in his father's funeral home in small-town Tennessee. As a makeup artist and gender illusionist—the term he prefers—he taught me more about writing fiction than I ever learned in graduate school. He told me that his goal in life was "to occupy as seamlessly as possible the space between male and female." I asked him if he'd considered a sex-change operation. "I've thought about that a lot," he said. "But if I became a woman then I'd just be a woman, and where's the theater in that?" While he was making me up I said, "Before we go out you'll have to show me how to act." With not so much as a tremble of the eyeliner pencil he said, "If you don't know how to act, I will have failed." And he was right: he created a character into which I had no choice but to step. Dolores Heitz, if you must know, and those of you who are familiar with the neighborhoods of San Francisco will get the joke.

My fictional marijuana grower and my real-life first cousin once removed are philosophers, and in his different way each is acting out a philosophy I've long held close to heart. Life is drag. It's not a question of whether to go in drag but which drag you choose.

And the fiction writer is a stay-at-home drag queen and the best among us are gender illusionists, putting on one character or another as the story demands. Nothing could be more restrictive or just plain killjoy than to place off-limits some ensembles of the infinite closets of the heart. A writer friend once told me that she allowed herself to people her books with characters from all races and genders but that writers' point-of-view characters should be limited to those they had personally experienced. In her case, that meant writing from the point of view of straight women. I was pleased, then, to read her latest novel and see that she'd challenged herself to write from the point of view of a gay man.

I was not at all surprised by her choice. From the first I have found writing from the point of view of women to be entirely organic, possibly because, youngest of nine children, I was largely raised by my four sisters. My first published short story was from the point of view of a woman—to embellish the point, a woman who is on her way to transgression, a Kentuckian beginning an affair with a man from "across the river," from the northern Yankee lands. Since then I have written from the points of view of straight men and straight women, a Bengali woman transplanted to the United States, a renegade marijuana grower, and a monk— though this last persona is so close to my heart that I ought to regard it not as fiction but as memoir.

It's a pernicious illusion of political correctness that writing from the point of view of someone of another gender or race or sexual orientation is somehow morally suspect—pernicious, because it presumes that what separates us is greater than what joins us together. In fact I find it hard to write from the point of view of the law, i.e., those who don't take pleasure in transgression—those who prefer the letter of the law over its spirit. I find it harder still to write from the point of view of someone born to wealth and power. I find it harder to write from the point of view of someone who doesn't revel in the created universe, independent of the shaping hands of humans. In writing my second novel I, an HIV-negative man, found it hard to write from the point of view of an HIV-positive man at a time when being HIV-positive carried a sentence of an ugly and agonized death. The greatest gap in the human condition, it struck me then and I still feel now, is not between nations or genders or races or sexualities but between the healthy and the sick.

I find it hardest of all to write from the point of view of someone who believes that life is supposed to make sense, that desire can be categorized and measured and weighed and calibrated.

To this end I recommend Richard Howard's recently published translation of Guy de Maupassant's last novel, *Alien Hearts*, not because Maupassant renders point of view in fantastically manipulated arabesques of both men and women (though he does just that) but because the impassioned tone of the novel speaks to me of a man writing under the gun. Maupassant had syphilis and had watched his brother go insane from the same disease before dying. More than once he tried to kill himself so as to avoid his brother's fate, only to fail and finally be committed to an asylum, where he died after eighteen months of agony. It is well for us to remind ourselves what everyone once knew but seems these days to have forgotten—that sex has always been risky, that pregnant women routinely died in childbirth, that women have always known that there is no such thing as "safe sex."

*

The vice president for marketing at a major New York publishing house told me some years back that no novel written from the point of view of an openly gay character, male or female, had sold more than ten thousand copies in hardcover. I found that fact worth pondering, since I take as a truism comedian Fran

Lebowitz's famous comment that if you removed Jews and gays from American culture all you'd have left is *Let's Make a Deal*. Why is it that presumably straight Anglo readers revel in reading about the cultures of African Americans, Hispanics, Native Americans, Asian Americans, but resist reading books about gay culture?

I think it has to do with sex, a topic which renders the American soul as uncomfortable now as ever. A generation of lesbian and (especially) gay writers has not helped this situation. In our necessary efforts to shake ourselves free of oppression, we conveyed the notion that gay culture was only or primarily about sex, a narrow interpretation that right-wing fundamentalists were too happy to reinforce. In fact gay and lesbian culture is about desire—not the same thing as sex—and desire is about the theater of life and, as its portable stage, the theater of fiction.

Maybe the resistance of mainstream readers to what I'll call a queer sensibility has to do with issues of certainty. America is a nation born of empiricists and we like our facts straight, so to speak. Facing what they perceived as wilderness, our forebears saw the imposition of order on chaos as our God-given calling. Americans have never much liked dwelling in the space between anything, most particularly the space between male and female. For if we cannot be certain of this basic "fact"—the "fact" of gender—what does that tell us about the rest of our carefully constructed illusions?

In writing this I realize that the law itself is a kind of drag, the imposition of a tailored suit over the crazy, tumbling, free-for-all chaos of life. I should make clear that by "the law" I mean not only that accumulation of precedent and power embodied in statute but the laws formulated by Aristotle and Newton and Darwin and Einstein. But Einstein was an outlier, growing closer to mysticism as he aged. In a letter sent six months before his death, he wrote, "For those of us who believe in physics, this distinction between past, present, and future is an illusion, however tenacious." It's the fiction writer's job to trouble that tenacity, to enable the reader, through this tenderest of devices, to penetrate the veil of what the Hindus call maya— illusion—and see through to the truth of matter, which is the fundamental unity and fellowship of all creation, including time and place, including most especially the human race.

Ordinary Acts
(1997)

Bless me, reader, for I have sinned: I have tried to keep a journal, and I have failed. The reasons for my failure are many and complex; among them may be laziness, but I think not. In my twenties, for something like five years I kept a journal more or less regularly, during which time I witnessed or read about events of great significance, e.g., the murders of San Francisco Mayor George Moscone and gay Supervisor Harvey Milk, the subsequent trial of the assassin Dan White, and the riots which followed the verdict. I look back at those journal entries and find them so juvenile and self-conscious as to be unreadable.

In *The House by the Sea*, one of her collections of journal entries, May Sarton writes,

> I find it wonderful to have a receptacle in which to pour vivid momentary insights, and a way of ordering day-to-day experience. . . . If there is an art to keeping a journal intended for publication yet at the same time a very personal record, it may be in what Elizabeth Bowen said: "One must regard oneself impersonally as an instrument."

My journal entries from the 1970s and 1980s were anything but impersonal—filled with polemic, directed at some imagined, recalcitrant reader whom I hoped to transform, through my deathless prose, into someone exactly like me. Looking back, I see that I was engaging in the rhetorical style of my Southern white male upbringing: assigning to my imagined reader opinions counter to mine, then arguing with myself while my reader listened. Writing, after all, is about constructing identity. For me, a journal never provided the necessary reality check—or the sense of an audience before which and for which I'm writing.

Letters were and are a different matter. Beginning earlier than my twenties—since I was old enough to write—I've used letters to record the passing events and impressions of my life. They present the advantage of engaging a known reader (my correspondent). The history my reader and I share lifts me out of myself; it reminds me that what I am about is not just expression but also communication. I write with intimacy because I know I am writing a friend, but I am bound by the discipline of letters to order my thoughts so that my audience may comprehend what I am trying to say. Excerpts from letters written during my lover's illness from AIDS or after his death later become central, critical passages in larger, longer works.

As I write I am in motion—500 mph at 35,000 feet, a place and a state of being I find conducive to writing; something about the stale, recycled air and the dog biscuit lunch, combined with that ineffable sense of being suspended in between, neither here nor there, the place where anything might happen even if it usually doesn't. I write in a Palmer longhand much deteriorated from the penmanship classes of my Catholic grade school days, letters which, on returning home, I enter into my laptop, print out, and mail, saving a copy for my files.

Returning from the journey to France during which my lover died, I wrote his eulogy, an unbearably hard thing to do, in the form of a letter. In a paroxysm of epistolary love, Barbara Kingsolver and I wrote each other monthly for several years, five- and six-page single-spaced tomes which covered everything from politics to literature to a mock marriage proposal which I accepted, and which I like to think remains in effect in some polygamous, parallel universe. Beware, however, of epistolary romance. A year later I carried on a similar, almost daily correspondence with a man who lived all of fifteen miles away, only to have the real relationship collapse the moment we had to communicate without cut-and-paste. Even so, at the risk of being thought crass I note that the romance served my writer's ends: it gave me the opportunity to record for a known audience my moment-by-moment experiences.

In this difficult, overcrowded, complicated, troubled time, it seems to me that simply to endure without descending into easy bitterness, to sustain some kind of hope and faith for one's peers and for those who follow—this is an achievement, an ongoing act of courage whose magnitude we too often take for granted. Journals or letters—these are means (may they endure and multiply) for declaring the significance of the small gesture: a record of the ordinary acts of life and love which bind us one to another, and which are our true source of hope.

God, Gays, and the Geography of Desire
(1995)

After eight children my parents had run out of ideas for names, so they gave me over for naming to the monks at the nearby Trappist monastery of Our Lady of Gethsemani. In the 1950s the Trappists more rigidly observed the rule of silence while practicing mortification of the flesh. They spoke only at prayer or in emergency; they slept on pallets in unheated rooms; they fasted on not much more than bread and water throughout Lent and on all Fridays. My father, a maintenance supervisor at a local distillery, delivered to the monastery the bourbon the monks used in the fruitcakes they baked and sold to raise money. The monks appreciated my father's studied casualness in counting the bottles; for his part my father preferred their company to the responsibilities of parenting his sprawling brood.

Within months of their acquaintance, some of those monks became regulars at our dining table. After running errands in town or through various subterfuges they made their ways to our house, managing to arrive just before supper. *They* got pork chops, *we* got fried baloney, but still as children we adored their company. For the most part they were educated men, Yankees from impossibly exotic places (Cleveland, Detroit), who stayed late into the evening drinking beer, smoking cigarettes, watching football on television, and talking, talking, talking.

Brother A. was fond of a fake grass skirt someone had sent my mother from Hawaii. When the moon was right and the whiskey flowing he donned the skirt and some hot pink plastic leis, then hoisted my mother to the tabletop and climbed up after. There she sang "Hard Hearted Hannah" ("the vamp of Savannah, G-A!"), while Brother A. swayed his hips and waved his hands in mock hula. Later he launched into Broadway tunes, warbling in falsetto with his arms thrown around one or more of his brethren.

Brother Fintan, my namesake, was a baker who made elaborate cakes for each of my birthdays until I was five, around which time he left the monastery for never-explained reasons. Years later he returned for a New Year's visit, accompanied by a handsome young man.

I was sixteen years old. I'd understood since earliest consciousness my own attraction to men, but in this I thought myself alone. Growing up gay in an isolated hill town, I had never encountered so much as a hint that others might share my particular landscape in the geography of desire. I understood this as the defining fact of my life: the invisibility of any resonant construct of passionate adult love. As a gay teenager I found nowhere a model for the love that most profoundly elevates; the love that so often fuels art; the love that finally underscores our notion of God; love whose nurturing and dissemination forms, along with familial and platonic love, the literal and spiritual heart of contemporary religion. As far as I was concerned, passionate love was something other people felt. In my quiet way I considered the books I'd read, the television shows and commercials I'd seen, my classmates' vocal heterosexuality, the models offered by my religion. I concluded that I was an aberration, one of a kind, an emotional eunuch with a heart of stone.

Then Fintan and his companion appeared. My family received them with its customary hospitality and enthusiasm and food and drink. More monks arrived to visit their old companion—there was dancing on the table; we trotted out the skirt and leis for Brother A., now in need of a stool to climb to the tabletop but otherwise as sinuous and campy as ever.

Afterward I listened for the customary post-party gossip. Had Fintan arrived with a woman, the household would have been abuzz: "Who is she? Might they get married?" Had he brought a mere friend, there would have been idle chatter: "Nice man. Needs a haircut." But: nothing. My namesake and his companion might never have sat at our table.

In my small town, among garrulous Southerners only one subject invoked a silence so vast and deliberate. That night I went to bed understanding that Fintan and his companion were lovers. Which meant that I was perhaps not the freak of nature I had until then believed myself to be; I was not alone.

I find something poignant and fiercely right in my owing, to my namesake and, in a manner of speaking, to the Roman Catholic Church, my discovery that this essential fact of myself—my sexuality; more than that, my capacity for passionate love—had a correspondent in the outside world; maybe even a name. Those who have survived adolescence: consider what it might mean at sixteen years old to be snatched into the light, the rabbit jerked from the dark hat of profound loneliness into an understanding that one is not alone, that one might love and be loved in fact in the ways that one's heart, soul, and body have already imagined.

*

All this, of course, has nothing to do with religion. Or has it? For a thousand years and more the Roman Catholic Church had reserved a place for me. Youngest son of a large family, introspective, intellectual, gay, I was the perfect candidate for what the French call *le donné*—the youngest child given (donné) to the religious orders, the family's gift to God. The sixties changed all that—instead of aspiring to the priesthood, I aspired to be a hippie, arguably a similar profession in different costume. Still: I was marked by the role, even as I evaded it.

I want to make emphatically clear that my rather extensive experience with the religious orders lends no support to the notion of cloisters or convents where sexuality runs rampant. I have no

idea and do not care whether the monks and nuns of my childhood were sexually active.* I know only that, by any reasonable
standard, many were gay men and lesbians, drawn to the institution that historically had provided them a place to retreat.

We're surrounded these days by folks who look back with vocal
nostalgia to what they imagine as times of religious harmony, lacking the fractious dissension and doubt that plague contemporary
Christianity. The harmony was a sham, of course, built on the mutual and collective participation in a lie. Everyone knew, had they
stopped to think, that some of the monks, and the Baptist church
organist, and the spinster librarian, and the close-cropped phys ed
teacher were gay. But no one stopped to think—society and religion depended on and enforced that deliberate thoughtlessness.

The emergence of lesbians and gay men into the light faces
contemporary organized religion with the challenge, never easy,
of accommodating truth. This is what makes it so exciting to be
gay *and* out in the 1990s—the simple fact of declaring oneself ad-
vances the cause of truth, so crucial to what George Eliot called
"the growing good of the world." Well into the age of technology,
who would have thought it possible to be a kind of Galileo? Yet
here we are, living, omnipresent evidence of a fact of life far more
obvious than the heliocentric planetary system—with Fintan and
his handsome companion, who needed a telescope?—but apparently just as difficult for Christianity to accept.

In looking at gays' and lesbians' place in Christianity, I want to
make clear my concerns: not the overpublicized arguments over

---

*A sentence written from idealism and woeful naïveté. Several years after pub-
lishing this essay, while researching and writing of *Keeping Faith: A Skeptic's Journey
among Christian and Buddhist Monks*, I was confronted with the issue of sexual abuse
by the clergy, both as a national scandal and specifically at the Abbey of Gethsemani. Almost fifteen years have passed since the publication of that book, during
which I have accumulated a deeper familiarity with Christian and Buddhist monastics. I remain convinced that the majority of religious, while as fallible as any
of us, are committed to conscientiously living out their vows. Readers interested
in my consideration of the relationship between sexual desire, religious vocation,
and a legitimate response to the sacred should consult Part II of *Keeping Faith*, in
the chapters entitled "Solitude," "Desire," and "Union."

public sex, or promiscuous sex, or the purported decline in morality, sexual or otherwise. Whether or not these issues warrant discussion, they apply to and ought properly to consider heterosexual as well as homosexual conduct. Throughout what follows I will limit myself to writing on Christianity—the only religion I know in depth. And, though Christianity provides individual spiritual guidance, I will limit myself to considering the public stance its organized, collective institutions preach toward sexually active gays and lesbians.

Along the way I will write as much of love as of religion. This is not confusion on my part but a deliberate focusing of attention where it belongs. For what is (or ought to be) contemporary, institutionalized Christianity but the communal celebration of love in its multitude of manifestations? Religion serves as the collective repository and arbiter of community morality, yes, but in Jewish and Christian history this has been marked by a progression from preoccupation with ritual and social custom (e.g., dietary laws, circumcision) to a more general concern with the importance of love as the foundation of human community.

What I am writing about what organized religion properly concerns itself with is the collective encouragement of the ways through which we express love for another, and our collective awe at the mystery that has brought us together. What I am writing about is the institutionalized exclusion of men and women, gays and lesbians from the religious community on the basis of one of those means of expressing love and awe. What I am writing about is not sex but love.

*

Like many lesbians and gays, I do not attend church, in part because I actively abhor the notion that any person might be expected to lower his or her self-respect to meet standards set by an external agency. I take no pleasure in writing this—my life, and by extension that of my community, is poorer for my lack of a collective acknowledgment of spirituality. But I am a Southern boy, raised with manners. I have no interest in crashing a party to which I have been so expressly disinvited. More to the point, through hard trial and labor I have earned my right to passionate love and to be loved passionately in return. I have in fact arrived at the heterosexual take on passionate love—I have integrated that love so wholly and completely into who I am that to deny it would be to deny my whole being.

As one who has decided to explore and express his spirituality apart from organized religion, I admit to some discomfort at finding myself arguing that organized Christianity must accept sexually active lesbians and gays, and that lesbians and gays should make that acceptance a priority in our struggle for equality. Why finally should it matter whether institutionalized Christianity accepts us as we are? We have our own churches, after all, for those who wish to worship, where our worth is assumed (as it should be) rather than considered something we must prove. The question is more than incidental, and broader in its application than to lesbians and gays. It engages at the most profound level the purpose of organized religion in all its forms.

Every day of my childhood the Roman Catholic Church set those questions before me: Where do we come from? What are we? Where are we going? (Their precise articulation I owe to Paul Gauguin, no stranger to Christianity.) Transmogrified cannibalism, mortification, exaltation—these were re-enacted according to a routine as dependable as sunrise and nearly (it seemed) as old. The church calendar was the literal expression of the cycling seasons. Lent: Fridays spent kneeling while the black-garbed priest prostrated himself before each station of the Cross, *Stabat mater*. Easter: transformation, rebirth, renewal, acted out in golden costume at midnight rituals, *Pange lingua gloriosi*. May, Mary's month: processions of girls in white, boys in blue, strewing flowers before a plaster virgin, *Salve Regina*. Corpus Christi: massive assembly in the high heat of summer to sing the praises of Christ's bloody wounds, *Tantum ergo sacramentum*. The cool touch of candlesticks, beeswax against the throat. The gritty rub of ashes on the forehead. Clouds of cloying myrrh ascending to the high-domed

ceiling. Mind-numbing mantras mouthed in a tongue at once centuries dead and more evocative than our quotidian English, *Ora pro
nobis, Ora pro nobis, Misere re nobis*. Ours was a sensual church, the
Opera of Faith, and we were its captive patrons.

I acknowledge the shaping hand with gratefulness. Because of it
I grasp in some way the incomprehensible magnitude of the mystery of being. Because of it I appreciate the importance of parable and ritual, storytelling and metaphor as our most appropriate
means to the invocation and expression of mystery. We cannot
know the answers to the questions which Gauguin so eloquently
poses; we can only ask. The history of religion in all cultures is the
ongoing expression of that asking.

In my small, backwoods hometown, religion was not mere social exercise but the necessary response, evolved over time, to the
paradox of the human condition: our collective attempt at recon-
ciling our place as self-conscious beings with an incomprehensible
universe. Human beings are animals that must ask why; organized
religion is our most democratic means of bridging the gap between that imperative and the unknowable void that gives birth to
the question.

To observe that institutionalized religion has historically preoc-
cupied itself with exclusion ("You may not belong to our tradition
unless . . .") is only to point up the greatest of its failings. Even now
religion continues to be one of the many ways (among them skin
color, nationality, gender, sexuality) through which human beings
categorize and discriminate; one of our ways of defining the Other.

The last several centuries of secular history have been an evolution toward an official recognition that such discrimination is
harmful to individual and communal well-being. I am arguing that
religion too may evolve, from an earlier preoccupation with particu-
larized theology to a place where its appropriate and necessary
role is to celebrate diversity—to establish, then strive for an ideal in
which we embrace our various ways of being "other" *within* community. Religion should define a moral structure which acknowledges
and promotes this yin and yang of the human condition: our place
within larger community structures; our uniqueness as individuals.

With its ages-old roots in collective experience and wisdom, religion is better suited than any other institution for this arduous and time-consuming task. For it to exclude any person of whatever sexual identity, or race, or gender, or nationality from participation in this collective expression of love and awe is to deny that person's humanity—to exclude her or him from the religious covenant. As the Roman Catholic Church acknowledges, no more significant exclusion exists. The application of that exclusion to whole categories of people reduces religion to social circle exercise, a country club with hymns and history, of no more significance than any secular institution embroiled in the politics of the accumulation and hoarding of temporal power and wealth.

*

For many years I described myself as having left the Roman Church, but I understand now that I misspoke. These days I say more accurately: the Roman Church left me. Rather than grant the existence of lesbians and gays and the courage of those who came out, it promptly tossed my brothers and sisters and me out on our ears.

In this the Vatican is hardly alone. Organized Christianity has failed lesbians and gays, at a time when we need access to the accumulated moral and spiritual wisdom of humanity as much or more than any segment of society. We are in the earliest stages still of creating a community—a stable set of values against which we may measure and reward or correct our conduct. Many of us are in the midst of battling to stay alive, or taking care of those engaged in that battle. Like all great religions, Christianity at its best can offer wisdom, lessons learned from the testing and tempering of values over time, which wisdom could be of priceless value to many lesbians and gays in facing our challenges.

Yet organized Christianity persists in its preoccupation with exclusion rather than inclusion. Churches, including those located in the heart of urban areas, where so many gays and lesbians live, turn their backs on us, even as they bemoan their declining congregations and participation. A gay friend—a longtime, devoted communicant—wonders aloud: What is wrong with this picture?

For our part, gays and lesbians have alienated potential allies in the churches by allowing ourselves to be defined not by how we love but by how we have sex. Gay publications, largely supported by advertising from bars, phone sex lines, and sex clubs, focus on bars, phone sex lines, and sex clubs. I write this not by way of denigrating those establishments—my family ran a tavern, and I'm a happy patron of many a well-run juke joint. But they have dominated our community's public persona, set the terms of our definitions of self-respect, and shaped our community morality, simply because until recently we have had no other institutions to fill those needs.

This is not the place for an extensive exploration of the relationship between morality and sexuality, except to say that they are intimately related. One has finally no more precious gift than that of one's body, and while some may give that gift more often and to more people than others, one loses sight of the connection between morality and sexuality at peril of one's self-respect, and by extension one's ability to love oneself and others. Not least among the arguments for welcoming lesbians and gays into mainstream religion is that such religions are or ought to be the appropriate institutions for the development and nurturing of individual and community values based on rituals, assumptions, and manners other than those formulated in bars and sex clubs.

*

In "Catholic in the South," I wrote of the contradictions and rewards of being raised in a flamboyant, Old World religion in the midst of the New World, Protestant South. At the time of its writing, I tried to grapple with issues of sexual identity, but each time I turned to the subject I was consumed with anger by the thought of the time wasted and lives ruined in the name of Christianity in general, Roman Catholicism in particular. Finally I set issues of sexuality and religion aside, hoping time would bring me to some more forgiving place.

I have not yet found that place, but more than anger at organized Christianity I now feel a consummate sadness that the wisdom it has to offer is lost to so many because of the ends to which
it has been turned by the unscrupulous, the ignorant, and those
confused and corrupted by power. Speaking of his symphony *Jere-
miah*, Leonard Bernstein argued that the great crisis of the twentieth century is the crisis of faith. The dominance of Christianity
by exclusionary, narrow-hearted men is the direct cause of whole
segments of America (hardly limited to gays and lesbians) dismiss-
ing institutionalized religion, once the cornerstone of the practice of faith in Western culture. This is a great tragedy, acted out
throughout gay and lesbian life. Taught to hate ourselves, denied
the ability to love fully and openly and with social approbation,
we turn to self-abuse (especially through drugs and alcohol) and at
times to abusing others.

I sympathize mightily with gays and lesbians who dismiss organized Christianity as at best a lost cause, at worst irredeemably
pernicious. I do not dismiss followers of so-called "fringe" New
Age religions, or the growing number of gay and lesbian converts
to Eastern religions. In these trends I see a legitimate effort to
satisfy—for people whom Christianity has failed—our elemental
hunger for a spiritual expression which celebrates our self-respect.

But for any foreseeable future, organized Christianity will
continue to provide most American children with what moral
instruction they receive, and to shape American social policy,
morality, and lives. It will continue to provide the majority of
Americans, regardless of their sexual orientation, their most
readily available vehicle in which to cultivate and practice the
virtue we call faith. Realism demands that gays and lesbians en-
gage institutional Christianity actively, if not in the churches at
least in secular forums. And that requires not sit-down, shout-
down activism—however necessary and effective that has been
and continues to be in other struggles—but informed, enlight-
ened discourse from open gays and lesbians who invoke the past
only and always in the spirit of forgiveness. For we cannot make
peace with ourselves unless we make peace with our pasts, and

we cannot make peace with our pasts unless we forgive without forgetting what religion has done to us.

I have not abandoned organized Christianity—though it has abandoned me—because I understand the power of religion to ennoble and elevate to a degree perhaps greater than that offered by any secular institution. I understand and appreciate its democratic appeal to our interior seat of mystery, which it touches and for which it offers expression. I want access to this experience for my people—I want it for all people.

*

In 1990 I helped my lover through his death from AIDS. From our first meeting I knew that he was HIV-positive; not long after our meeting I learned that I was (as I remain) HIV-negative. The disparity of our situations was the source of great anguish, much of it centered around the possibility, however remote, that he might infect me. Among my friends and family many never understood and still do not understand how I could have subjected myself to such risk; one straight friend accused me of having "a romantic death-wish."

I can only answer that I was in love. I had been uplifted, transformed. Had I refused this love—the most profound yet given to me—I would be a vastly poorer man. I think of Chekhov's wife, the famous Russian actress Olga Knipper, who chose to live with and marry him when it was clear he was dying of tuberculosis, a disease more contagious than AIDS and at that time both more mysterious and nearly as fatal.

In caring for my lover I came to understand the tautological relationship between God and love. My lover's love for me and mine for him made me into something better, braver, more noble than I had imagined myself capable of being. I was touched by the literal hand of God, for this is what love is, in a way as real as I expect to encounter in this life. I may be forgiven some impatience with those who would ascribe to that sacred experience anything less than spiritual dimensions of the highest sort—the domain, in a word, of religion.

In various essays and in a *New York Times Magazine* profile, Lewis Thomas suggests that humanity may evolve spiritually as well as physically, adapting (he hopes) to an understanding of the world that makes more room for community virtues and values. Is it so farfetched to see the struggle of gays and lesbians for acceptance in mainstream churches as another step in the maturation of Christianity? What gays and lesbians have to teach the larger religious community is a profound understanding of the necessity of love, in all its infinite permutations and manifestations.

I like to think that gays and lesbians may perform for organized Christianity our customary role of defining the cutting edge. In this case, agitating for acceptance in mainstream denominations pushes further the historical shift in Christianity's concerns away from the particular and toward the general—away from concern with, for example, theologically correct methods of baptism, and toward a focus on the preservation and propagation of love, which is to say the manifestation of God in our time.

Why do I suppose that gay men and lesbians may have some special access to understanding the nature and importance of love? Because no one knows the value of something better than those who have struggled to achieve it. Denied love from without, our challenge has been to create it from within. This is no easy task, and is not accomplished by the simple declaration of the wish that it come true. Like all struggles of any significance, the fight for the right to love and be loved is ongoing and omnipresent, and manifests itself in every act of every day. Our reward is, or may be, a fuller understanding and appreciation of what others so often take for granted.

*

My sister sends a black-and-white photograph taken on my fourth birthday. In it I'm seated before a vast cake made in the shape of the head of Mickey Mouse. Rendered with painstaking verisimilitude in vanilla and chocolate icing, Mickey Mouse is nearly as large as I. Chin resting on one fist, I preside over it with the contemplative air of a young mystic. Along with the photo, my sister sends a saucer-sized medallion made from wheat paste, the centerpiece of my first birthday cake, which has survived the depredations of time and insects. On it there's painted in pale blue and ochres an elaborate Virgin and Child, one of Christianity's most potent symbols of love.

These works of culinary art came from the hand of Brother Fintan. They are evidence of his greatness of heart, the boundlessness of his love, large enough to encompass me and my immense family and the young man whom he brought to meet us that New Year's Eve.

Gays and lesbians, brothers and sisters, are finding our ways to spirituality; we are making communities across America and around the world. That we would do so sooner and more effectively with the assistance of organized Christianity I do not doubt, but we live in the here and now, we do not have time for the women and (mostly) men of Rome and the various Protestant denominations to open their hearts to the community of love. I write in celebration of what I see happening in meetings and community actions and hospices and service organizations and yes, churches. I write in celebration of the spirituality I see explored and expressed in its multiplicity of ways, in a community to which I am proud to belong. I open my arms to it and through it to the world, an act of faith in life and in love.

In Sophocles's *Oedipus at Colonus*, Oedipus speaks to his daughters:

I know it was hard, my children—and yet one word
Frees us of all the weight and pain of life:
That word is love.

Over two thousand years later, Oscar Wilde will write, "God's law is only love."

Religion's proper concern is the preservation and propagation of love, which is to say the manifestation of God in our time.

Beyond Belief
(1998)

What we have to be is what we are.
—Thomas Merton

The chapter room at Our Lady of Gethsemani, the rural Kentucky abbey where Thomas Merton wrote, is long and narrow and, on this pleasant evening of July 1996, filled with monks. Along the right wall, under an image of the risen Christ, stand our Trappist hosts, the "white monks," dressed in white albs covered with black hooded cowls and cinched at the waist with broad leather belts. Next to them stand the Benedictines, the "black monks," the more publicly engaged, apostolic of the Catholic contemplative orders. Among these monks are scattered a few women, most dressed in the white blouse and below-the-knee gray skirt favored by post–Vatican II nuns. Along the left wall, under a batik banner of the seated Buddha, stand the Buddhist monks—the Mahayanists of Tibet wearing maroon, the Southeast Asian Theravadans wearing saffron. A lone Japanese monk wears dove-gray robes trimmed in black and white; a lone Taiwanese nun wears saffron, peach fuzz sprouting from her newly shaven head. Among these Asians mingle the American Buddhists—what are those nice Jewish women and men doing wearing black Zen robes? Except that some aren't Jewish and some aren't Zen, some are wearing street clothes, and some of the Asians are now Americans, immigrant priests and monks whose Buddhist congregations increasingly include white Americans. The Christians and the American Buddhists are almost all pale as parchment; the skin tones of the Asians range from Japanese ivory to Sri Lankan browned butter. Timothy Kelly, abbot of Gethsemani, and the exiled Dalai Lama of Tibet stand at front center, focal point for the Gethsemani Encounter, this international convocation of Buddhist and Christian monks, nuns, and contemplatives conceived in 1968 at the Dharamsala meeting between Merton and the Dalai Lama. Within the month Merton would be dead, electrocuted by faulty wiring in his Bangkok hotel room, but his proposal of this convocation gestated until here we are, here I am, a self-styled skeptic among mystics.

Geography is destiny: European and Asian ways of being first mingled in the aptly named Middle East, which served both as incubator and melting pot of the West's great spiritual traditions: Judaism and its children, Christianity and Islam, with all three influenced by Asian philosophies (Zoroastrianism, Buddhism) transported, along with silk and spices, over the great trade routes. Now in America the "circle [is] almost circled," to quote Walt Whitman, and the two great ways of being are meeting again: the westward-migrating, Jewish- and Christian-rooted democratic idealism of eighteenth-century Europe is encountering the eastward-migrating perspectives of Buddhism; the Enlightenment is encountering enlightenment; the religion of the Word is encountering the philosophy of silence. Observing from the back of the chapter room, I am brought to ask if the encounter of these Western and Eastern disciplines may hold the key to a legitimately American faith.

Faith: not at all the same as belief. American Zen philosopher Alan Watts explains the difference:

> Belief . . . is the insistence that the truth is what one would 'lief' or wish it to be. . . . Faith . . . is an unreserved opening of the mind to the truth, whatever it may turn out to be. Faith has no preconceptions; it is

a plunge into the unknown. Belief clings, but faith lets go. . . . Faith is the essential virtue of science, and likewise of any religion that is not self-deception.

My travels among American monasteries have brought me to write not about belief but about faith; not about doctrine (the Virgin Birth, papal infallibility, reincarnation) but about the subsuming of self to the greater order. I am setting out in search, not of an American religion, but of an American faith.

Watts contends that belief in God is antithetical to faith, because God, conceived as omnipotent power, necessarily stands between ourselves and complete letting go. To argue as much is to dismiss the role of belief as a means to the end of faith. Usually expressed in metaphor (the burning bush, the resurrected Christ, the reincarnated essence of being), belief challenges the imagination to conceive and embrace a universe larger than what we immediately perceive. Among other roles, it engages a community in a collective imaginative act, one of the most powerful ways of binding a people into a collective identity.

Which is where the trouble begins. When communities use belief not as an aid to faith but as a means of establishing identity, sooner than later the guns appear. Catholic, Jew, Protestant, Sikh, Buddhist, Hindu, Muslim—these are powerful labels, easily used to identify and take up arms against the Other. This is the challenge facing contemporary institutionalized religions if they are to be vehicles for peace rather than for dissension and violence: the teaching of belief as the outer garment to faith, a means to the end but not to be mistaken for (and finally not essential to) the real thing.

But what is the real thing? The question itself is central, the path of this journey. For skeptical Americans, children of a nation born of the union of religious idealists and Enlightenment rationalists, what does it mean to have faith?

And so I return to the monks, the keepers of faith.

*

Monasticism is among the oldest of human archetypes; like the
family, like marriage, like the complex, interlocking rituals of
sexual desire, it predates recorded history. It is less a manifestation of any particular religious tradition than an outgrowth of
the human imperative to ask why. It is the practice (practice: the
methodical pursuit of perfection) of the search for a state of integration with the whole of being that Buddhists call nirvana, that
Christians call a state of grace. It offers a discipline to govern and
assist the search for faith.

Theologian Ewert Cousins speculates that monasticism arose
almost simultaneously with the individuation of consciousness—
as soon as humans perceived themselves as individuals apart from
their community, a few panicked at the notion of a fate distinct
from that of their tribe or clan. They ran for the hills and the
caves, to give their lives over to contemplation of the mystery of
being alive and alone. Monasticism does not exist in cultures (trib-
al Africa, New Guinea, Native America) where individual identity
is subsumed to the community. It emerges when and where cultures recognize the possibility of an individual consciousness and
destiny apart from the communal whole.

That monasticism is so ancient complicates the definition of the
term; across history the word "monk" has been used to describe
a wide range of individuals and practices. In the West, our words
"monk" and "monastic" contain and express solitude (from ancient Greek *monos*, "one alone").* And yet in both West and East,
the practice evolved from the earliest wandering hermits (eremites)
to become communal (cenobitic). In the West, the Benedictine orders (of which the Trappists are a subset) abide by the Rule of St.
Benedict, composed in the sixth century with a presumption of
cenobitic life. In the East, Buddhist monastics observe the precepts
of the vinaya, with its roots in the earliest Buddhist teachings and
similarly oriented toward a collective life. Still, the essence of the
practice springs from an ongoing engagement with the terrifying,

---

* Following the practice of many contemplatives, I use the term "monastic" to
include both men and women, and "monasticism" to include all contemplative
orders, regardless of the gender of their members.

liberating knowledge that finally we each face our gods and demons by ourselves. Thousands of years into the history of monasticism, the novice Trappist enters the walled-in enclosure at Gethsemani under an engraved lintel reading *God Alone*.

In various forms and at various times some version of the ascetic life has manifested itself in all major contemporary religions, but it achieved its apotheosis in Buddhist and Christian monasticism. Buddhism evolved directly out of monasticism—Siddhartha Gautama, the sixth-century-BCE Hindu prince commonly referred to as the Buddha, began his interior exploration by joining one of the small bands of mendicant ascetics who roved (and rove) the Indian subcontinent. Even today traditional Buddhism posits that enlightenment—defined as triumph over samsara, the endless cycle of desire and dissatisfaction—may be achieved only within the sangha, a word broadly translated to mean the monastic community.

In contrast, the Bible (Old or New Testament) contains no explicit references to monasticism. Christian monks describe their life as an attempt at a literal imitation of the life of Christ, but the first monks of the Sinai, who lived as hermits, had as much in common with distant Indian ascetics as with the infant hierarchy of Christianity. The history of the Western evolution of the practice is complex, but a simplified version has the hermits' students establishing communities so as to live near their teachers; from these communities evolved the powerful abbeys that became tools for the advancement of the Vatican's temporal ambitions, and that in the Middle Ages were often synonymous with politics and intrigue.

For a brief period in the early centuries of Christianity most men and women monastics saw the discipline as a paradigm for all humanity—their expectation was that all Christians would live in communes. But even at its numerical peak monasticism remained the exception rather than the rule. Considered in their kindest light, however, monasteries offered both West and East a model of a simple, contemplative life to inspire the larger secular world. They are communities where property is shared and time, freed by collective labor, given to contemplation and prayer; exemplars of a life lived not for the future but in the here and now, a life built on and lived by faith.

In the ideal, at least, that function continues, but with some notable exceptions the practice of monasticism is in decline. As culture secularizes in both East and West, monasteries have emptied. American monastic populations peaked in the 1950s, as people fled or rebelled against World War II or the Korean War, or attempted to come to terms with their aftermath. For those men and women, midlife questioning coincided with the tumultuous sixties, and they left the cloistered orders in droves—Gethsemani, one of the world's largest Trappist monasteries, had almost 250 monks in 1953; now there are fewer than 70, with a median age nearing sixty-five. In Asia, monasteries are holding their own mostly where they are perceived as opposing a repressive regime (as among the Tibetans in exile), or where (as with Buddhist monasteries in Myanmar, or Catholic monasteries in the Philippines) they retain their position as a relatively easy meal ticket in a desperately poor country.

Paradoxically, as monastic professions have declined, American interest in the contemplative life has intensified. Persons wishing to reserve rooms for retreats at Gethsemani must phone from six months to a year in advance, and Eastern/Buddhist meditation centers are similarly booked up. That explosion of interest owes itself partly to the aging of the baby boom generation; the hippies, having made their livings and raised their children and now facing mortality, are returning to the big questions of their youth, in an attempt to define and honor what is sacred in an overwhelmingly secular culture. But the growth in interest in Eastern philosophies also reflects dissatisfaction among Americans with mainstream Judaism and Christianity, with their emphasis on belief—on doctrine and dogma.

Monasticism is the archetypal manifestation of the impulse to mystery, an institutionalized response to the intuitive need to construct and dwell in sacred time. What's remarkable is that, though separated by vast gaps of geography and history and culture, both Western and traditional Eastern monastics lead lives committed to poverty, celibacy, and obedience, addressing the three great obstacles to faith, the cornerstones of contemporary secular culture—money, sex, and power.

*

The first great principle of Buddhism also explains the success of the consumer economy: Humanity is born to *dukkha*, "dissatisfaction" (often translated as "suffering"). Stated simply: we are born to want what we do not have; if we get what we want, we transfer our desire to another, less attainable object. Starting from this principle, Buddhism teaches how to recognize and defend against human weakness; capitalism focuses our intelligence and creativity on its exploitation.

At a panel discussing the explosion of Buddhist references in pop culture, designer Milton Glaser posed the question: "In a culture where every image or idea can and will be used for commerce, how can anything remain sacred?" And if nothing sacred remains, why not lie and steal? When we're barraged with messages equating personal worth with material wealth, when the poorest of the poor can buy a gun, what's astonishing is not that America has so much violence but that it has so little—testimony both to some elemental human attraction to virtue and to our willingness to fund a police state as the price of prosperity. Meanwhile, fundamentalist movements grow here and abroad, as people seek to find or restore value in lives corporate capitalism perceives as another resource to be exploited, exhausted, and trashed.

Monasteries as repositories for the sacred—it's a charming if slightly desperate hope, at least if one compares the relative numbers of monasteries and Walmarts on the American landscape. Then I spent time in monasteries, to discover that they're less islands in the culture than microcosms of it—whatever is happening "over the wall" is generally epitomized inside it.

As in mainstream culture, the technology that severed Trappists from their roots has enabled them to prosper, to the point where a Gethsemani Trappist told me, "We have too much money. We've become the worst thing possible for men of faith—we're bourgeois, respectable men of substance, making a living."

*

In the weeklong Gethsemani convocation of people dedicated
to contemplation, many of whom are committed to celibacy, the
subject that most frequently recurs: anger. The subject that never
occurs: sex. Rocket scientist on both subjects, I ask: Might there be
a connection between the obsession with the first and the evasion
of the second?

Possibly more than any other aspect of monastic life, celibacy
intrigues, mystifies, and (often) repels lay people, and for good reason. In the knees, in the heart, in the head, sex renders us weak—
the wisest and strongest among us understands what it means to
be a fool for desire—and to be weak is to be comically, tragically,
poignantly human. To remove oneself from sex is arguably to separate oneself from one's humanity, to place oneself in a class apart
and above. Power inheres to the party who says no; unless undertaken within a larger context, celibacy can be a kind of power play,
and the institutions of religion—East and West—have historically
used it to that end, creating a priestly class apart from and presumed to be superior to those who are sexually active.

Which is too bad, because monasticism in both traditions can
speak eloquently to matters of sexual morality and discipline.
Most of us, most of the time have sex not to make babies but to
assuage desire—not just hormonal desire but the desire to love
and be loved, for union with the whole, for an end to the aloneness
inherent in being alive. During sex, to invoke a Christian metaphor, we die to ourselves, however briefly; to invoke a Buddhist
principle, we have a moment of surcease from samsara. We are
one with ourselves, with another, with *the* other; we triumph over
solitude, even over death. And then it's finished, and we're alone,
and dissatisfaction returns.

Monasticism seeks not to triumph over aloneness but to embrace it (*God Alone*), and in so doing to transform the short-lived
triumph of orgasm into an ongoing triumph of consciousness, an
enduring acceptance of and union with the whole great roundness

of being—including birth, growth, love, insecurity, loss, aging, suffering, death. This is the place where desire becomes faith, springboard for the poetry of John of the Cross and Sor Juana Inés—both monastics, both mystics, troublesome to their traditions while alive, valued once dead, writers of poetry that invokes spirit and flesh, in which faith is not an etherealized concept but another manifestation of the crazy, fooling energy that drives the heart (among other organs).

"Chastity does not mean abstention from sexual wrong," wrote the British novelist and Roman Catholic G. K. Chesterton. "It means something flaming, like Joan of Arc." I prefer the Buddhist concept of "right conduct" to Chesterton's "chastity," but the point remains the same: what finally is at stake is not sex but love, and celibacy is or ought to be not about punishing that but sacralizing it, celebrating it, bowing down before its power in an effort to channel and focus that power to constructive ends.

Traditional monasticism is very good at disciplining the power of the mind; in the face of the power of the body, it has folded its tents and resorted to proscriptions more arcane in traditional Buddhism than even Roman Catholicism. The rise of feminism and the concurrent consciousness of the body has rendered that contempt for the flesh no longer possible. Monasticism faces a fork in the road: in one direction lie reaction and fundamentalism; in the other, the labor of reforming the practice of celibacy to acknowledge and respect the body and its needs.

*

Among the official participants at the Gethsemani convocation, men greatly outnumber women; among the observers—sitting in the rear but not allowed to participate—women significantly outnumber men. Excepting the American Buddhists, this interfaith assembly presents a picture postcard of religious hierarchy, East or West: the men elevated on the dais, the women below and to the rear. Later in this week a Sri Lankan Buddhist priest takes the microphone. "To be sure I understand," he says. "In your tradition,

women are considered inferior to men." A Trappist priest illustrates with a gesture, not judgmental but merely graphic: hands
extended, one at his shoulder, the other at his waist.

Jesus Christ and the Buddha share this: they based their teachings in universal democratic principles. Athenian democracy limited citizenship to freeborn men; Jesus Christ and the Buddha
preached philosophies equally available and applicable to all—
man, woman, rich, poor, citizen, slave, saint, sinner. The Buddha
transcended the rigid castes of his native India; Jesus welcomed
not just lepers and pagans but (most astounding for the time)
women. True democracy begins in the West when Jesus embraces
Mary Magdalene, in the East when the Buddha accepts his stepmother's plea to permit women to form monasteries.

Their revolutions remained intact for as long as it took for their
teachings to be institutionalized. Though the Buddha yielded to
his stepmother's plea, he insisted on conditions that made clear
that nuns occupied secondary status to monks; beginning with his
successor, Buddhist precepts codified those conditions. The perse-
cution of Christians in the West kept Christian doctrine and structure fluid (and remarkably egalitarian) until Constantine's acceptance of Christianity in 312 CE. But with official sanction came
institutionalization, with Augustine, Western history's other most
famous monk, as its architect.

As single-gender communities, monasteries East and West have
offered opportunities for women that existed nowhere else; some
of the abbesses of the Middle Ages are among the most powerful women of history. But both traditions have operated within
and helped sustain a patriarchal culture that regards women/nuns
as second-class citizens. Buddhist or Catholic, monasteries have
functioned as highly organized economic units that have historically served the ends of power (in this case, the religious patriar-
chy) as much as those of faith.

The bloody severance of church and state accomplished in revolutionary France and the secularization of government throughout Western Europe all but wiped out monasteries in the West.
However brutally accomplished, the removal of monastics from

political influence is surely the most beneficial modern development for the practice. Because Christian and American Buddhist monks are removed from temporal power, they represent their traditions' best opportunities to preserve, explore, and enhance the cultivation and practice of faith.

Power and faith do not comfortably cohabit. Belief—that is, dogma and doctrine—may serve the ends of power, but faith is the province of individuals, not institutions. So long as individuals have something to lose—the Buddhists would say, so long as we have attachments—it's difficult to accomplish the letting go that is faith's sine qua non; the more we have to lose, the greater the challenge. To find genuine faith—to find those who dwell in the world as it is, rather than as they would have it be—one must look among the poor, among the dispossessed, among the outsiders to power.

Sister Maricela Garcia was born in Mexico to a poor family and spent years in a teaching order before seeking out the Trappistines. Olive-skinned, dark-eyed, a García Lorca woman, she shines with a fierceness that brought her to be transferred from her Trappistine monastery in northern California to Gethsemani for three months that have become three years, in which she has lived as the only woman among an enclosed, cloistered community of seventy men. "What are we doing to awaken a questioning attitude in the people who come to us?" she asks.

> We wear a dress from the twelfth century that stands up because it's so dirty but we can't take it off because we'll be naked. That's us not wanting to change, fearing change and not understanding our own worth. . . . Change is always uncomfortable. To me the obvious issue is: We're dying out. We're no longer a living tradition. Younger people are thirsting for a spiritual life, and we're not doing our job in offering it to them.

*

Each of us must find for ourselves our wellspring of faith. To judge from their devotion to Mary, many women find that place through their gender; for me it resides in the source of my otherness, my homosexuality.

Father Matthew Kelty, one of Gethsemani's older and most popular counselors and openly gay, speculates that "gays have always dominated the religious life because it was a viable way of living. I would think that in the Middle Ages most were gay, though they didn't call it that, of course. Look at the monasteries of the Middle Ages, which were centers of art, culture, peace."

Instead of "gay" a younger speaker than Father Kelty might use the word "queer"—persons who may be homosexual or hetero-sexual but who define themselves as outsiders, who haven't the luxury to assume a world the way they would have it be and so must construct a philosophy for embracing it as it is.

Of course not all those who live responsibly at the margins of power are gays or lesbians. My point is that, as repeatedly noted in the Old and New Testaments, the outsider has special access to faith, if only because he or she grapples daily with limitations imposed by circumstances, whether of class, race, gender, sexual orientation, or physical, psychological, or intellectual limitations. Because a healthy society recognizes the need to moderate hubris, it takes care to protect and listen to its outsiders, who function as a combination of court jesters and advance scouts (as in Sophocles or Shakespeare) for the culture as a whole.

In its earliest incarnations, this was one role of monasticism: to act as an institutionalized contradiction of and conscience for power.

*

Monasticism is like art—in a very real sense it *is* art, the hours of life shaped to an ideal, never achieved but always present as a place to which to aspire. Like art it must be an end unto itself; its beauty and its truth reside in its being explicitly nonutilitarian. It is about making time sacred, removing from it any possibility of a price. But like all that is sacred, contemplatives dwell in and are of the real, physical world, and a vital monasticism is committed to ways of living out the truths of that physical world through monastic life.

The Trappist writer Thomas Merton's greatest achievement may lie not in his books but in his lifelong, largely successful battle to shift the focus of the Trappists from penitence to devotion, from asceticism to the preservation and enhancement of the sacred. In keeping with his aspirations, the goal of monastic reform should be to rediscover, not reinvent, in their purest forms the permanent ideals of monasticism, which may act as a model for a more materially frugal, spiritually engaged life—a living out not of doctrine but of faith.

I like to think that an American faith would define the place where skepticism may coexist and collaborate with a respect for mystery. I like to think that faith, in its infinitude of expressions, is that quality that might keep us humble, in the face of our inevitable hubris; it could enable the transformation of knowledge into wisdom. I like to think of monasteries as repositories of faith and so as both models and catalysts to which we can look for inspiration in shaping the vessels of our lives.

This is the great contradiction between our economics and our political and spiritual aspirations: capitalism excels in offering choice, but liberty fulfills itself not in choice but in discipline. Life is like water—it takes the shape of the vessel into which it's poured; remove the vessel and it's lost. What we are seeking is a vessel into which to pour the chaos of life; what we are seeking are models of discipline.

Not that contemporary culture has no models to offer. Corporate capitalism offers the considerable discipline of making money. In *The Varieties of Religious Experience*, William James invokes the discipline of military life, which is still available to young people. But both military and corporate disciplines rely on "the need of crushing weaker peoples," whether they are the assemblers of silicon chips in the Philippines or the strawberry pickers of California or the leftists of Grenada, whereas monasticism based in agriculture or in cottage industry offers a model of a sustainable discipline.

New millennium or no, the mass of people is surely no more likely to flock to monasteries now than in the time of Augustine. The rare young man who joins the Trappists today is likely to have been raised in those few remaining American pockets of fervent Catholicism, and is likely to be more conservative than his elders. The monk who spends three or six months at Tassajara, the San Francisco Zen Center's monastery and hot springs in the heart of California's Coast Ranges, is likely to be a college-educated liberal with an income, if not to burn, at least to sacrifice. At both institutions nonwhite people are notable for their absence.

But ideas percolate through society in mysterious ways—consider how Zen concepts have permeated popular culture even as its practitioners remain a tiny minority. The Benedictine monks of the Middle Ages expressed their faith through the discipline of the illuminated manuscript, their love of the Word rendered incarnate. Looking from the cliff above the organic farm at the Zen Center's Green Gulch, I see in its meticulously patterned fields of vegetables and flowers a twentieth-century equivalent to those pages, the love of the earth given shape and form and substance. Writing almost a year later I am dogged by the memory of that farm, and by the young people who told me how it drew them to Buddhism before they knew anything of Buddhist practice or philosophy.

Might Gethsemani's acres of bottomland—now leased out to a corporate farm—be turned to a similar end, with young people brought to reconnect with the earth? Could the hundred-plus Christian monasteries scattered across the American countryside act as loci for a revitalized discipline of a particularly American faith, incorporating the wisdom of the federalists, the feminists, the activists for human rights and dignity, and functioning as places of collaboration between skepticism and spirituality? The idea presents immediate objections, chief among which is the challenge such outreach poses to the solitude and contemplation that are hallmarks of monastic life. But it's hard to be complacent among the young—from experience I can write that it's hard to be complacent on a farm—and an authentically lived monastic life should be above all else the antithesis of complacency. I would like to think that the revitalization of American Christian monasticism might incorporate some return, however small-scale, to the Trappists' historical roots in agriculture, or—in the case of the Benedictines—to their historical roots as cultivars of culture. These practices—farming, scholarship, teaching—are the literal incarnations, after all, of the roundness of being.

This is a big demand of small institutions whose populations are generally shrinking and elderly. But in East and West, the history of monasticism is a repeating pattern of spiritual engagement followed by decadence followed by reform and renewed engagement. I like to think that the example of the American Buddhist contemplatives and monks might inspire the American Trappists not to imitation but to a new reform built on a Western version of an engaged, contemplative, American faith, incorporating democratic principles while de-emphasizing doctrine, integrating body and spirit while bringing to the forefront the veneration of the simple mystery of being.

In his profile of the encounter of American Jews and Tibetan Buddhists, *The Jew in the Lotus*, Rodger Kamenetz suggests as much for American Judaism; why not American Christianity? The Western spiritual tradition needs not a wholesale conversion to Eastern traditions but a return to its authentic, egalitarian, faith-based roots as articulated in all the gospels, stripped of the institutionalized church's centuries of obsession with temporal power and prestige.

*

This is the continuing gift of the New World—the breathing space to challenge the old ways of being and doing. Emerson, the great prophet of the American faith, asked, "Why should not [Americans] also enjoy an original relation to the universe? . . . Let us demand our own works and laws and worship." Transcendentalism,

Emerson's particular ideal, withered on the vine, even as its Eastern-influenced principles significantly shaped American spirituality.

Like Emerson, monasticism poses an ideal—a community of people identifying a discipline and attempting to live it out. The practical effect of American multiculturalism has been to challenge the old shared values without offering viable substitutes—in effect, to fracture the big picture without providing an alternative. Instead of looking to turn the calendar back, might Christian monasticism, influenced by the American Buddhists, propose a new ideal: a discipline of faith lived in respect of and in collaboration with the disciplines of skepticism? I pose the question to Christian monasticism because it is of the West and because it is our rich and entirely adequate cultural heritage.

In *The American Religion*, literary critic Harold Bloom argues persuasively for the existence of a uniquely American religion, the product of the individualistic American character. But American religion without American faith is fundamentalism—religion grounded not in faith but in belief. I argue for aspiring not to an American religion but to an American faith, founded in and cherishing the old wisdom, but also actively testing that wisdom in the crucible of the present moment, our present nation so far removed in history and character from its worthy roots. Already every established denomination in the United States (including Judaism, Catholicism, and Buddhism, and soon, I suspect, to include Islam) sustains a practice distinct if not separate from its Old World origins. In this American faith, belief—that is, doctrine and dogma—takes a distant back seat to faith in oneself, in one's place in and responsibility to the workings of the great order (if one insists on a word: God), in the ongoing task of the preservation and enhancement of the sacred.

Speaking before a congress of monks in Bangkok, in remarks given a few hours before his death, Thomas Merton argued that

> what is essential in the monastic life is not embedded in buildings, is not embedded in clothing, is not necessarily embedded even in a rule. It is concerned with this business of total inner transfiguration. All other things

serve that end . . . I believe that by openness to Buddhism, to Hinduism and to these great Asian traditions, we stand a wonderful chance of learning more about the potentiality of our own traditions.

In my early thirties I first undertook to write about faith, but each time I took up the subject I was assaulted by bitterness at the thought of all those lives ruined or deformed in the name of organized religion. As I grew older I was better able to embrace the gift my church gave me—an appreciation of mystery, the experience of awe. But it was meditation, learned from the Buddhists, that brought me to some kind of forgiveness. These days I set aside a half-hour daily as sacred time; these days I am beginning to imagine what it means to have faith. I have taken years to begin to become familiar with Eastern traditions, and those years have served to educate me into the vastness of my ignorance. But they have taught me as well my right and responsibility to shape the Western tradition into which I was born to my particular place and moment in history. With time I may be able to name myself, if not a Catholic, at least a Christian.

*

Several months after the Gethsemani convocation I talked with Norman Fischer, abbot of Green Gulch. "A fully developed imagination enables us to live in a world that's ennobling without dwelling in some fantasy land," he said. "For a Buddhist, enlightenment is the development of the faculty of imaginative vision that enables us to see the world in a transfigured way." He looked up from his black Zen robes. "That's what a Catholic Mass is about, right?"

The Mass: You enter the Gethsemani Abbey church, high and long and narrow, whitewashed brick, plain as an empty hand that directs your eyes forward to the dais, on which sit two vertical blocks of black granite topped by a horizontal black slab, lit from above by a single spotlight. Behind this altar stands the starkest of thrones: six flat planes (a back; a seat; two arms; two armrests) of polished oak. To either side: ranks of monastics, robed and cowled.

You have entered the theater of faith. The setting prepares you for blood sacrifice; what you get is art. It is 1,998 years into the Christian era, six thousand years into the era of self-consciousness, and we are here to bear witness to the triumph of the imagination, the great human achievement: the acting out of mystery in metaphor instead of in fact. Transubstantiation: the bread becomes flesh, the wine becomes blood, we eat the flesh and drink the blood and so reenact the violent heart of the mystery of being.

To teach literal transubstantiation as the focal point of this genuine miracle is to take the narrowest point of view on the greatest work of ongoing performance art Western civilization has conceived. It is to collude with secularism in assigning the miraculous to the past, when in fact the spark of the divine resides in the present imagination, in the leap of faith required to conceive and achieve science, art, the Catholic Mass. It is that facility and faculty of imagination that is the genuine and continuing miracle, that organized religion so often suppresses as an obstacle to the ends of institutionalized power.

I take an imaginative leap here, to see consciousness as evolving from those first monks hiding out in the hills and caves of India through Plato, who understood unity with the whole of being as the soul's aspiration and goal. We move from the era of prophets who ascribe the mystery of being to external agents (gods and demons) to prophets (Buddha, Jesus) who direct us to the sacred place within. We move from an era when the acknowledgment of mystery demanded blood sacrifice (less than five hundred years ago, the Aztecs built a brilliant civilization around it), to an era where we are clever enough to substitute bread and wine and understand it as the real thing. The quality we draw upon to accomplish this extraordinary imaginative leap—this act of confidence in our human right and responsibility to shape the terms of our encounter with the divine, as well as confidence in the greater order in which our search takes place—we give the name of faith.

Must rationalism reject faith? "Science without religion is lame," wrote Einstein, "religion without science is blind." Contemporary physics is arriving at the realization that mystical writers, often monastics, repeatedly present as the culminating fact of the contemplative life: the understanding that science and art lead to mystery. Finally we can only glimpse the great unity, with an understanding increasingly supported by scientific evidence but finally sustained by a leap of faith. Immersed in and part of this great river of energy, we live every instant the precise analogue of the moment of transubstantiation in the Catholic Mass, in which the divine order is at once revealed and concealed. Seen in this light, faith does not divide but unifies body and spirit, perception and miracle, science and spirituality.

Faith is first among the cardinal virtues because every virtue proceeds from it, including and especially love. Faith is the leap into the unknown, the entering into an action or a person knowing only that you will emerge changed, with no preconceptions of what that change will be. Its antonym is fear. In the prosperous 1990s America is a fearful society (consider our obsession with security, whether national or international, or in our financial, professional, emotional, and spiritual lives) because we are a faithless society. Without faith, without that willingness to embrace life, including its uncertainty and pain and mortality and mystery, the soul becomes stagnant—possibly the only aspect of the universe that can resist change, and in doing so possibly the only aspect of the universe that can really die.

Faith accepts that we cannot know everything and can control only a little. If we can bring that acceptance to science—if we can recognize science as existing on a continuum with art, if we can embrace both not as means to the accumulation of money, sex, and power but as undertaken for the sake of the love of knowledge, which is to say the love of beauty, which is to say the love of truth—we will have reason to hope.

*

In paling darkness the *shuso* makes her circuit through the Tassa-jara canyon, ringing the wake-up bell with the self-satisfaction of a young woman already up for an hour and given the pleasure of rousing everyone else. In silence your neighbors struggle into their black robes. Outside a waning moon sets over the dark ragged line of the mountains, egg into nest, the moonlight knits shadows of branches on a glistening carpet of wet leaves. The black-robed monks hurry to the meditation hall, where later you will join them, but on this particular morning you walk past the hall and up the canyon, beyond the kerosene lamps. You follow your nose past sage and under California bay laurel to the sulfurous spring, heat-ed in the bowels of the earth. You drop your clothes and step in.

An early-sprouting big-leaf maple drips catkins into the chill. A middle-aged man (pudgy at the waist, thinning at the crown) rises from the pool. He arches a hand over his head, first to the right, then to the left, then he bends at the waist, then straightens, stack-ing his vertebrae one at a time until his head lolls back, to one side, then another. He raises his arms and you see stiffness rising from his ruddy steaming skin, crepuscular light passes through the curl-ing steam and it's as if an angel has stepped from the cold rushing stream below through the heated waters and into the brightening dappling light, and for a moment you are given to understand that you are that man, that angel above the rushing water, that here and now you are made in the image of the divine, that paradise is a mirror in which you see yourself, that what we have to become is what we already are.

Part IV

Witness and Storyteller
(2008)

I've just returned to my home in Tucson from four months in France and the transition from the Champs-Elysées to Speedway Boulevard is a little rough and so I find myself at the gym in mid-afternoon of a Friday on the theory that at least my body should derive some benefit from my spiritual torpor.

Space, we have space in Arizona and so my gym's floor is a vast acreage with enough room between machines to accommodate a Manhattan studio apartment. Even after months away I recognize a few faces, including that of a singularly beautiful young man who is seriously into pumping iron. I'm a middle-aged professor at the local university with my interest confined to age-appropriate guys but this particular man possesses a beauty that is tough to ignore ("Young man," Blanche says in *A Streetcar Named Desire* as she caresses the paperboy's cheek, "young, young man"). But I feel the pressure of all that land and moral rectitude between me and the nearest coast and so I keep my eyes largely to myself.

I finish my workout early—the spiritual malaise infects the corporeal—and I head for the locker room, which recently underwent expensive renovations, with the only noticeable change being larger mirrors framed in cheesy tan and ochre tile. There I encounter the beautiful young man, whose locker turns out to be next to mine. The room is empty except for us.

He's wearing baggy sateen gym trunks in the school colors of the university where I teach—bright red—and a white cotton singlet of the sort favored by men of the Americas. As I enter he's standing in front of the floor-to-ceiling mirror, pulling up his singlet with one hand while running the other across his muscular abdomen. I pass him en route to my locker and give him not so much as a nod but he takes note of my presence. He returns to his locker and strips off his singlet in one smooth sweep of his arms, then returns to stand in front of the mirror while I go about changing into street clothes.

He's moderately tall and has the complexion of the west of Ireland, rose and translucent even in this harsh neon light. Six more ounces of muscle and he'd be overdeveloped but whether from youth or by choice he hasn't reached that point. He stands between the mirror and me so that we cannot meet each other's eyes and begins to run through poses rehearsed not for the stage but for himself and now, evidently, for me. Smooth-chested, a tangled mop of brown hair matted with sweat, his scarlet trunks low on his hips, he flexes one biceps, then a second, then both, then his pectorals—I know because I steal glances at his back and I know how anatomy works, the back muscles clench in this certain way. The air smells faintly of urine and mold and thickens with desire— my desire for him, his desire for himself, his desire to be desired. For five minutes and more he strikes poses, occasionally running a hand over a knotted muscle, while I look while pretending not to look. The only sound is the drip of a leaking shower head and the hiss of the steam room.

All history floods into this moment—my lonely and sex-starved youth, the years of shame, the coming to terms with shame, the beautiful men and a couple of women I have held in my arms and who have held me in theirs, my great love dead in midlife, my many years alone, my growing old alone, my impulse to say something fine and astonishing that will mark the moment not by way of seduction but by way of defining and controlling this tidal wave of history and testosterone and middle age and shame and the knowledge that my dick is in my throat, anything I choke out will be stupid and tinny and false and that words, those beautiful traitors to love, will break the spell. Who is this man, what is this moment about? What remains of my youth wants an answer and wants it now: *Is he gay? Is he putting on this show for me? Is it possible here in Tucson, out in the remote middle of nowhere, that he can be oblivious to the eroticism of this fairy tale, this daydream?*—even as an older and wiser voice says: *This is it. The moment needs no definition, it defines itself, it is what it is. There is no time, we are outside of time, there is no place, time and place are illusions, there is only this. What you see is what you get. Keep your big writer's mouth shut.*

An older man enters—seventy-plus, I would guess, bald and wrinkled and shirtless and paunchy. He stares frankly at the boy. "Looks pretty good to me," he says. The boy wilts and blushes—with someone else present I can look at him openly now. He mumbles a thanks and makes for his locker and pulls on his clothes and leaves.

The troll has entered and broken the spell, a sentence I write not at all from contempt for the troll—I am closer in age to the troll than to the boy and getting there at more or less the same rate as all of us in the great democracy of time—but in recognition of the mythos of the moment: Narcissus gazes into the pool rapt in love with himself, amazed that he can be in love with himself, in love with being in love with himself, in love with the power of his beauty until Pan comes along to muddy the waters. A thing ain't happened till it's been told—the words of an old moonshiner from my native hills come to mind, and my place is to be witness and storyteller, as vital and necessary as the act itself.

Shrines and Wonders
(2016)

In 1894, a rural Kentucky entrepreneur sold New York businessman A. W. Dennett the frontier log cabin in which he claimed
Abraham Lincoln had been born almost a century earlier. To
quote Mark Twain, "How singular! Yes, and how lucky!"— since
Dennett parlayed the cabin into a business, transporting it around
the country for exhibition as the original Lincoln home. Each time
the cabin was broken down and reassembled, it lost an inch or
two to the process; after several years of touring, it was placed in
storage, considerably worse for the wear.

Then a committee of leading Americans, among them Twain,
President William Howard Taft, Ida Tarbell, William Jennings
Bryan, and Samuel Gompers, came together in a campaign to
build the cabin a suitable home. To draw up the plans, they engaged John Russell Pope, later the nation's leading neoclassicist,
architect of the Jefferson Memorial and the National Archives
Building in Washington, DC.

Pope designed a Greek temple for the Kentucky woods, a massive structure of rose granite and marble, rich in numerology (one
step for each year of Lincoln's life; a column for each of the original colonies) but with a problem: the display room was too small to
accommodate the cabin for which it had been built. Pope designed

his monument to house not a real log cabin but a romanticized cabin that conformed to his conception of Lincoln's humble origins. But the corpses of history must conform to their tombs, so the sponsors lopped off several more feet of the cabin in order to squeeze it into Pope's mausoleum.

That same Yankee businessman had simultaneously "found" the birthplace cabin of another Kentucky native—Jefferson Davis, president of the Confederacy. The Davis cabin joined its Lincoln correspondent on the tour around the nation, but in the breakdowns and moves from one site to the next, the logs from the two cabins became mixed. Current investigation has established that the oldest logs in the "Lincoln cabin" (or "Davis cabin," depending on your historical perspective) date to the 1840s, meaning that the logs of the cabin enshrined in the Lincoln Birthplace National Historical Site symbolize less the birthplace of either president than a celebration of capitalism's skill at serving our imagination's urgent need to be validated.

Is there meaning to be found amid the murky facts surrounding the mud-chinked cabin that a wily Kentuckian assembled from logs he claimed to have found scattered about the original Lincoln farm and that he sold to a gullible—or enterprising—Yankee businessman? Or in that same businessman's "discovery" of the logs of the Davis "birthplace cabin"? If the highest aspiration of human culture—of science and art, history and memoir—is not *fact* but *truth*, where does the story of the Lincoln/Davis "birthplace cabin" fall?

*

Here, far from prying eyes, surrounded by cohorts of
holy angels, you are rewarded by being ravished seven
times daily . . . transported among the celestial choirs
to listen to their sacred music.
　　　　　—François Petrarch, *Elegy of the Magdalen*

This trade in relics is an old business—second only to you-know-what, our oldest business, with the oldest and second-oldest trades converging in the story of Mary Magdalen. Provençal legend has the Jews of Palestine condemning the Magdalen and her fellow disciples to their fates by setting them afloat in a small barque without sail or rudder. After uncounted days they drift ashore a thousand and more miles west, near the mouth of the Rhône River. All but the Magdalen crisscross Provence proselytizing and performing miracles—the disciple Martha charms into submission the Tarasque, a monster that has been terrorizing the village of Nescul. The villagers stone the now-docile animal to death, then as an act of repentance take the animal's name as their own (today's Tarascon) and give it a place of honor on their coat of arms.

In fact the disciples' rudderless boat could never have negotiated the treacherous Mediterranean; in fact only a few years after the death of Jesus these disciples would have considered themselves Jews, not Christians, but the greedy mind is asking questions instead of being present to the story and so I give it stern orders to shut up. Sin is always more interesting than virtue and in Provençal legend the Magdalen is the reformed prostitute who became Jesus's devoted follower.

The legend reinforces a thousand-year-old confusion that persists into contemporary times. Of the Magdalen the canonical gospels tell us only that she was a devoted disciple of Jesus and that she followed him to Jerusalem, where she helped take him down from the cross and was the discoverer of the empty tomb and the first to see him after his Resurrection. She is traditionally identified as a prostitute, but nowhere in the New Testament is she referred to as such. She is traditionally identified as a sinner, but the "woman which was a sinner" (Luke 7:37) is never named.

Sinner or saint, our Provençal Magdalen makes her way from the Mediterranean to the forests of the interior mountains, "long sacred," according to my guidebook, "to the Ligurians," the region's prehistoric tribes who were massacred or who assimilated into the communities of their Greek and Roman conquerors. There she spends the remaining thirty years of her life in contemplation in a cave high on a cliff. She is buried locally and revered until the eighth century, when the Saracens overrun Provence and her bones are dug up and hidden from their depredations. Five centuries later Charles of Anjou, looking for a way to boost the local economy and to reinforce his kingdom's claim to legitimacy, arranges to "discover" those bones, now located many kilometers distant from the Magdalen's cave. He builds a cathedral to house them—the basilica at Saint-Maximin-la-Sainte-Baume—as well as a shrine at the cave itself.

The story is familiar and ancient—seeking to obliterate a local cult, an upstart religion appropriates its holy places and fabricates a myth in keeping with its own ambitions—but here you and I enter the narrative. I go on these pilgrimages in homage not to relics, but to the imagination that calls them into being. I go to remind myself of my roots among these pilgrims who still come by the thousands, many of them Roma ("gypsies"), stateless outcasts for whom the Magdalen is patroness.

And so in the heart of winter I drive inland from the Provençal coast to the cathedral at Saint Maximin, a drab affair interesting mostly for its introduction of Gothic architecture into a part of the world where Romanesque prevailed. The skull of the Magdalen, preserved in a glass jar in the cathedral's crypt, is worth a shiver, though a more emphatic chill awaits with the small cylinder of glass in which floats the scrap of flesh said to be the spot where the risen Christ touched her forehead.

From the cathedral I drive south into the mountains to the Magdalen's cave. Halfway there I almost turn around—I hadn't thought the journey would be so long, the road is winding and treacherous but I am drawn by "this forest, long sacred to the Ligurians . . ." The road is a white-knuckler, barely wide enough for one car. The countryside is fantastically deserted, in stark and pleasing contrast to the tourist-mobbed coast.

At the grotto trailhead there's a hostelry with a gift shop. The trail skirts a muddy field before plunging into the forest, which is immediately and satisfyingly deep, a cathedral whose ceiling is the intricate web of the oaks' bare branches and above them the winter-blue sky. At this altitude the mossy oaks shelter blackberry canes and small pines but as I climb the pines give way to mottled beeches and the oaks acquire mistletoe garlands in their highest branches. Soon, even at midday, I am in the shadow of la Sainte-Baume, the holy mountain. I walk on for a mile and then another, up and up until I reach the stairs at the foot of the shrine. The bone-white cliff rises hundreds of feet straight up, with the shrine to the Magdalen built into its vertical face.

I climb the steps and for the first time encounter other tourists, a couple who ignore the signs requesting silence and gab in mellifluous French. How we are given to chatter like sparrows, how noteworthy that silence requires a conscious act! How much of our talking is a flight from demons when so often the demons, masters here as elsewhere of sleight of hand, live in the beautiful, treacherous words themselves . . .

Inside the grotto, the cave lit only by candlelight. Even the chattery couple are hushed to whispers. The only sound is water dripping one drop, then another, from the ceiling to the floor. Scattered about are statues of the Magdalen in sorrow or in meditation or in ecstasy—legend, commemorated in Petrarch's poem, has angels transporting her seven times daily to the heavens to listen to celestial choirs.

The grotto offers a sweeping view across the plain of Provence, punctuated by Mont Sainte-Victoire, beloved of Cézanne, and in the farthest distance Mont Ventoux. The cave is an extraordinary feature, a gaping mouth in the middle of the cliff's vast vertical face. Little wonder that it was sacred to the Ligurians and their successors—it sets itself apart, calling: *Climb to me, enter me, make a story to explain why I am here.*

*

Some years ago, researching a Bengali character for a novel, I took myself to Calcutta, now renamed Kolkata, for Durga Puja, one of the world's great festivals, held every year in late October, with precise dates determined by astrologers. Every civic group and residents of every neighborhood are assessed—on occasion extorted—to finance a pandal, an elaborate structure constructed of hemp, one of the principal crops of Bengal, woven over a bamboo frame and housing an altar inside. These pandals range in size from modest—comparable to a small American suburban home—to palatial structures. Often they are outlined in multicolored, flashing electric lights, and woe to the government if power is not reliably sustained across the festival's ten days.

The city's lowest caste works a full year building the pandals and their altars, working with hemp and clay from the Hooghly, the branch of the Ganges that flows past the city. The design and execution of the altars varies as wildly as human imagination but their characters are as consistent as the Virgin, Babe, Ass, and Ox of a Christmas crèche: Durga rides her lion, her four children arrayed to either side, brandishing weapons in her ten arms as she defeats the evil demon Mahishasura, always rendered as a blue water buffalo, the last form he assumed in his vain efforts to escape. On the tenth day, to mark the turning of the wheel of time, the altars are removed from their elaborate settings and paraded to the river, where they are set afloat, mud returning to mud so that the timeless cycle can begin anew. The pandals are destroyed by way of celebrating the new year, in which the calendar is wiped clean and the world and its peoples begin afresh.

Recently an American chain hotel located on the fringe of Kolkata preserved a pandal and its altar from the great festival, so that business visitors at other times of year might enjoy the experience vicariously and perhaps, seeing an example of its fantastic elaborations, return at Puja time as revenue-producing tourists. Encountering a Durga Puja altar on the hotel grounds is like visiting an Atlanta or San Francisco Hyatt in July to encounter an elaborate Christmas crèche. The encounter is even more incongruous because the point of Durga Puja—the point of returning all that work to the river from which it came—is to celebrate impermanence, the constant flux of the universe in defiance of our efforts to fix it in place.

*

Halfway around the world, not far from my Tucson home, a folk shrine is dedicated to the story of a man caught in flagrante delicto with his wife's mother and murdered by her jealous husband. El Tiradito—"the outcast"—has become a pilgrimage site for supplicants of all kinds, among them women seeking a good husband, heartsick persons wishing for healing, and border activists protesting the latest migrant atrocities. Visitors write their wishes and prayers on papers that they stuff in crevices in the adobe bricks at this, the nation's only shrine to an adulterer.

The visitor may be standing on US soil, but the animating imagination, which knows no borders, is of Mexico. Only now, as I revisit these pages, do I realize that El Tiradito may embody why Americans are so afraid of our complex, fascinating neighbor to the south—its cheerful and unreserved embrace of mystery, its cheerful and unreserved embrace of death.

*

At cocktail parties in San Francisco and New York, I occasionally declare with conviction that I really believe that Jesus rose from the dead, in part because I delight in getting a rise out of people in a part of the world where empiricism (some might say cynicism) is the local religion and in part because, with Lewis Carroll's White Queen, I submit daily to the discipline of believing "six impossible things before breakfast." "Discipline?" you may ask. Yes, because as much as the most ardent empiricist, my grabby reason *wants* the universe to be tidy, it *wants* life to make sense, it *needs* to believe that whatever can't be explained today is waiting for the right measuring stick to be explained tomorrow.

Does the universe exist to be explained, to submit to rules of grammar and syntax which presume and impose a man-made order on reality—the only word, wrote Vladimir Nabokov, that ought always to be enclosed in quotation marks? Or is knowledge a tool—a means to wisdom, but not to be mistaken for wisdom itself? The Indian filmmaker Mira Nair has said that she relocated to the United States because she wanted to live and work in a place where the films made sense. Almost any Bollywood film illustrates what she left behind, but where is the law dictating that the universe must lend itself to explanation by that bunched mass of synapses and neurons and blood vessels we call the brain? Is it possible that Bollywood films, with their nonsensical plot twists and random interventions by deities, more accurately embody "reality" than, for instance, *Avatar* or *Zero Dark Thirty*?

To ask if Durga really had ten arms, or if the Buddha was really born from his mother's side, or if the Red Sea really parted, or if Jesus really rose from the dead, is to ask the wrong questions. These stories are koans—they arose to remind us of the importance of faith, the virtue that enables us to keep going on the days after, say, a grim cancer diagnosis or the burning of your home in a wildfire or the upending of a life by substance abuse, to name three traumas that have recently made themselves known in my life or the lives of those I love. The miracle stories exercise the imagination ("six impossible things before breakfast"). If we are to liberate ourselves from our desires it will not be through facts alone but through our imaginations—through our capacity to imagine, for example, a world in which prosperous nations lead the way in modeling a simpler and more efficient life, in which the rich voluntarily yield some of their wealth and power to the people whose labor made it possible.

I'm an amateur naturalist—"amateur" in the sense of its etymological roots ("one who loves"). I read *Nature* and the *New York Times*'s Science Tuesday, occasionally *Scientific American*, and I have a large bookshelf of popular science titles and guidebooks in subjects from geology to ornithology. If I understand what I read correctly, current theories posit that the great majority of the universe consists of something (dark energy? dark matter?) whose nature we don't understand, but whose existence physicists predicate because without it, our theories of what we do understand fall apart.

In college chemistry I would have been flunked for plugging in numbers to balance my equations, but I'm an avid follower of the physicists' theories because I situate science at one end of the spectrum of art—glorious art, mouth music we make up and sing, like sparrows chattering, so as to fill the void and declare our presence and every once in while hit on some beautiful and true note or song.

Contemporary physicists' story of the origins of the universe may serve the same function as those koans, so long as one understands them as another in a long history of the many beautiful stories we tell ourselves. Harmony and a judicious skepticism regarding skepticism itself require at least tolerance of those who believe in a causality other than physics, or those who believe in no causality at all, or those who believe that faith worthy of the name requires that we transcend reason without abandoning it.

*

Belief is easy, the postmodern rationalists tell us, it's skepticism that's hard, and for the longest while I was on their side—in my skeptical college years I would have dismissed the story of the Magdalen's relics and grotto or of the Lincoln/Davis "birthplace cabin" with a world-weary sigh, grateful for the triumph of reason that, among its many other gifts, liberated me from the anti-Semitism and homophobia of my Christian ancestors.

But now I recall the parable of the talents, in which the master rewarded the servants who took risks and punished the servant who played safe. To those who are given few talents, belief is enough—religion or science, the means to the end hardly matters; what matters is an unquestioned confidence that life's great questions have answers. But for those who seek faith—who have been educated into the geology and biology and into the dark, bloody story of humanity's slow progress, who know our institutions' long histories of abuse and betrayal—to possess all that knowledge and *still* to have faith surely requires the greatest heart, the greatest risk.

Leaving India, at the Kolkata airport I found some rupees in my pocket, so I bought a phone card and called my aged mother. She was understandably mystified that in late middle age her youngest child would take off for a month in, of all places, Kolkata. She asked, of course, about my impressions of the place. Without a moment's thought I said, "How generous are people who have nothing, how stingy those who have everything!"—an observation born of my six weeks' stay and from which, I am sorry to say, I do not exclude myself. Reason would have us clutch to our chests that which we call ours—nation, property, money, spouses, children, self. Generosity requires a more mysterious gesture, growing from an instinct biologists are struggling to explain, only to produce along the way as much beautiful theorizing and befuddlement as physicists face when confronting that vast unknown required by Einstein's theories.

Sometimes I think the mysterious force we call gravity is just another name for love, the force that pulls us down and back to the dust from which we came. After all, "all bodies (with mass) in the universe are drawn to each other no matter how far they are apart"—you see, the elemental forces inspire even Wikipedia writers to eloquence, and don't you love the little cherub hiding behind the parenthetical phrase? What bodies are *without* mass? And what might be the implication for the domestic and foreign policy of the most powerful empire in history, were it to acknowledge and respect the gap between those who insist that life submit to reason and those who believe in and inhabit a numinous world?

Reverence and Irony: On Beauty and the Sublime
(2016)

The ticket is torn, the velvet rope pulled aside, and I am admitted into one of the most remarkable rooms in the world—the entrance gallery of the Uffizi Gallery in Florence, an ornate salon the size of a basketball court that displays front center exactly three paintings: On my left, the *Rucellai Madonna* by Duccio, painted in 1285 CE. On my right, *Maestàdi Santa Trinità* by Cimabue, painted between 1280 and 1285 CE. Directly ahead, chief among equals, *Ognissanti Madonna* by Giotto, painted in 1310 CE.

The *Rucellai Madonna* by Duccio: A large (12' x 5') painting on wood, it presents a flat, two-dimensional goddess seated on a golden throne, holding the Christ Child. With huge, lidless eyes she engages her audience with a profound, penetrating gaze. Her throne is supported by six angels, arranged in two columns of three angels each. One angel appears to kneel on another's head who in turn kneels on the head of the third, and all are painted in the same flat plane as the Virgin. She wears dark blue robes gilt with gold and fit for a queen, but not inhabited by much in the way of a body—the dark colors conceal the underlying anatomy, transforming it into a single smooth plane. One knee thrusts tentatively forward, but it's lost in the folds of her dark robes and so far below her waist as to raise the question of anatomical correctness. The background is pure gold, real gold, gold-leaf paint signifying a world not at all like that of our daily lives but instead the sacred world of mystery, ruled over by a mystical God whose very naming diminishes him; a God who can be known only in unknowing, who can be reached by no human prayer but only through the intercession of the Mediatrix, Queen of Heaven.

Cimabue, *Maestà di Santa Trinità*: A large (12' x 7') painting on wood presents a goddess more richly clothed even than Duccio's, but she's a goddess with a human touch—where Duccio's Virgin holds her child stiffly in what passes for a lap, Cimabue's Virgin gestures at her seated child; a hint of a smile plays around her lips. Her feet peek from the hem of the rose-and-gilt robes, tentative but incontrovertible evidence of the body beneath. As in Duccio, angels range up either side of her throne, but these angels are crowded together, the round golden halo of one blocking the torso of another. They wear placid, ethereal expressions but they're jostling like riders on a rush-hour subway; they're becoming flesh-and-blood humans and so have to grapple with the body's awkward demands for elbow room.

Giotto, *Ognissanti Madonna*: A large (11' x 7') painting on wood presents Mary, the very flesh-and-blood mother of the child Jesus. She wears a mantle—blue, of course, over a white gown—but her simple, elegant clothing approximates the dress of one of the wealthier wives of Florence's growing middle class; these clothes are observed rather than imagined. With one hand she steadies the child in her lap. Both breasts, full with milk, and both knees push against her robe's white folds, which reveal rather than conceal her contours. Here again the angels crowd around, but some all but obscure others; unlike in either Duccio or Cimabue, they're presented in half-profile. Giotto is trying to represent what the eye sees, no more and no less, so that he paints only the aspect of the angels that faces toward the viewer, not the side that faces away—a back side that will disappear from Western painting until Cubism restores it in the early 1900s. The angels in the rear are painted on the same scale as those in front, but the distinctly three-dimensional throne has a front and a rear, drawn along invisible lines projected backward toward what would soon be codified as a vanishing point—the West's embrace of perspective, and with it the invention of modern Western painting, is just around the corner.

I'm slack-jawed, moved to tears in the presence of these beauties and the transition they represent in barely thirty years from the age of faith to the age of reason—from painting as an expression of mystery (Duccio), to painting that attempts to capture the world in which we literally live (Giotto). The implications for our experience of the sacred are profound—seven centuries later we are still grappling with the passage embodied and expressed in these three paintings.

I have crossed an ocean to see this, to understand with the eye how and when and so, perhaps, why we in the West chose to privilege observation over imagination, analysis over contemplation, mind over spirit, duality over union, irony over reverence, skepticism over faith. And I'm standing there and standing there, until a small woman with big hair arrives at my side. I have been traveling alone for almost two weeks during which I've hardly spoken to a soul, and in my eagerness to spill some small part of my awe at the splendor and mystery before which we stand I turn to her, but before I can speak she heaves a great sigh and with all the eloquence of feet that have walked too far over too many parqueted floors to look at too many paintings she says in the resonant accent of the people, *my* people, "We-l-ll, don't they all look just alike."

A moment passes, then I say in what I hope is my most respectful tone, "Ma'am—they don't all look alike, and if you'll give me a moment I'll tell you why." She nods apprehensively but stays, rooted to the spot by the memory of some elementary school reprimand, while I set forth as gently as I can what's so remarkable about this assemblage—why one of the world's greatest museums chooses to devote the whole of this palatial room to three paintings, why it has chosen these as its calling card, the introduction to the crowded rooms to follow. I point out the glorious artistry but wooden expression and looming eyes of Duccio's goddess—not at all "natural" eyes, not because Duccio could not paint more "natural" eyes but because he had no intention to make them "natural."

Quite the contrary; in their largeness and darkness they're meant
to draw us in, an effect heightened by the lack of perspective—
there's no distance between her and us, we're all dwelling in the
same plane. Like the figures in all icons, she casts no shadows but
emanates light—she is less a woman than an archetype, a sacred
figure recognizable as such by perhaps any person in any culture,
Christian or otherwise. Cimabue is painting from that same tradition but he's begun observing the human beings around him and
he is trying to *represent* them, albeit firmly within Duccio's Byzantine tradition. Giotto defines the break: one foot firmly planted
in the age of faith, the other with equal firmness in the coming
age of reason. The shepherd's son miraculously discovered by one
of Florence's leading teachers, Giotto was trained as a sculptor
before taking up painting, and his frescoes and panel paintings live
and breathe with his farmboy-turned-sculptor's struggle to express
in the two-dimensional medium of painting the fullness of the
solid, three-dimensional forms he has held and shaped with his
hands. In his work we see the beginnings of a "scientific," rea-
soned approach to painting—art based in careful observation, that
will ultimately lead to the paintings of Leonardo da Vinci and the
physics of Isaac Newton and Albert Einstein, with all that these
imply for how we perceive and inhabit the world.

"Wow, you've really studied this stuff," says my audience of one,
and I'm flattered at the compliment but feel obliged to demur.
"Really, at some point I just started to look, really look." I happened to have arrived at that point courtesy of Zen Buddhism, but
before I mention that she politely edges away.

Nowadays we look at these Madonnas and we say, *Ah, Giotto's is the
most realistic—look, he's figuring out perspective!*—when what we ought to
say is that his Madonna most closely corresponds to our modern conception of the triumph of reason and the subjugation, if not outright
disappearance, of the sacred. Duccio's contemporaries—for whom
the sacred was firmly fixed above reason—might well see *his* Madonna as the most "realistic," in that it better honors their sense of the
proper order of the universe—God as mystery, God concealed in a
cloud of unknowing, represented on Earth by His Mediatrix.

Art, under which term I include writing, gives expression to the order that resides in what appears to be chaos. Note that in this way of thinking the artist is not imposing order; he or she is uncovering an implicit order. Our word "cosmos" derives from the ancient Greek word for "order"; Duccio lived in a world in which that order was as fixed and assumed as the golden sky that backs his paintings and many of the sacred paintings in the Western world for the preceding millennium. Do we suppose Duccio painted his skies gold because he couldn't find blue on his palette? No, he painted them gold because he intended to suggest a world other than that which can be perceived and calibrated and measured. When Giotto turns the skies blue, is it any surprise that thunderclouds follow?

In the world of the three painters we've just visited, the visual arts were the common cultural medium, the most democratic means of conveying information—few people knew how to write or read, but peasants came to the cathedral to "read" stories illuminated in the stained glass and illustrated by paintings and statuary. With the invention of moveable type and the cheap, widespread availability of books, the printed word rapidly replaced visual art as the lingua franca, and the visual arts began their long move uptown. Removed from their vital purpose, they became wall decoration.

Then in 1853 Admiral Perry sailed American gunboats into the harbor of Tokyo, in a government-financed expedition to bully the Japanese into opening their economy to foreigners. Shortly thereafter Japanese and Chinese art flooded the French art market. Trained in the heavy, "realistic" style of the École des Beaux-Arts, Western painters marveled at the light, airy, self-consciously abstract brush strokes of their Asian counterparts. Van Gogh was influenced by Buddhism, whose principles served as midwife for his particular style. *Le japonisme* became the rage among French painters, even after the establishment came and looked and sniffed. "Impressions," declared some deservedly forgotten critic, but the label stuck.

One could make the case that the Buddhist understanding of art and "reality" liberated the Western visual arts from the illusions of objectivity. What's beyond dispute is that le japonisme liberated Western painting to a place where, sometime after Van Gogh, a Spanish artist with an anthropologist friend could lower himself into a cave in the southwest of France and perceive the truth and skill and glory in what many before him had discounted as adolescent graffiti—elaborate paintings portraying the hunt, not at all realistic and thousands of years old, men and women and elk and bulls and blood and death. His name was Picasso.

*

One of the ultimate questions at the heart of the human condition: Do we believe in progress? Do we subscribe to what the great Russian doctor, author, and social activist Anton Chekhov, a writer known for his frank, unsentimental rendering of the human condition, called "the unceasing movement toward perfection"? I'll take up that question again, but I interrupt myself to define terms. What is "perfection"? What is it that we hope to be moving toward?

For my purposes here I take my cue from Plato and define perfection as Beauty, with a capital B—because maybe Plato got it right. Maybe we are drawn toward union with the One, with "the One" being some primordial, deoxyribonucleic memory of the moment of creation. Maybe all that matters is the search for Beauty, with Beauty defined as the integration of the self and the world, the disappearance of ego, the union with each other in the One—in Buddhist terminology, no duality, no separation, or, as St. Paul would have it, we are all one in Christ Jesus, drawing, or so I believe, on the Greeks who drew in turn on the Buddhists with whom they'd exchanged ideas in the course of Alexander's conquest of India.

The impulse to make art and the impulse to make science arise from the same source, which is the desire for union with the One. Whether artistic or scientific, the impulse arises from desire. At its most superficial level we could label this the desire to *know*, whether it's to know why Madame Bovary committed suicide or why time only runs in one direction—if in fact it does. But at the heart of our questioning is the desire to recreate and inhabit the original moment of creation, to return to that moment when we were all one with the One and no division existed between reason and faith, mind and body, you and me, our selves and Beauty—or if you prefer, God, though if Beauty must have a name I prefer the response from the burning bush when Moses had the temerity to ask (Exodus 3:1-14): the vowel-less, unpronounceable sigh of the wind, YHWH. Or, in the formulation of Native American writer N. Scott Momaday, the Great Mystery. Or, in the formulation of that Anglican-priest-on-the-lam Charles Darwin, the Creator.

Every great work of art exists in conversation (sometimes in argument) with that original unity. Therefore mystery lies at the heart of every great work of art, including that greatest work of art, the universe itself.

Reading or listening to cosmologists talk of the moment of creation is like listening to a delightful fairy tale—in which the artist or scientist is in effect reenacting that original moment of creation, which will always resist our efforts to have it make sense. It will always resist the application of reason.

Neither physics nor art nor any human endeavor, including theology, can answer the big questions. But they can *address* the big questions, and in the distinction between "answer" and "address" may lie our salvation. Nobel-winning physicist Steven Weinberg writes in *The First Three Minutes*, his meditation on the origins of the cosmos:

> The more the universe seems comprehensible, the more it also seems pointless. But if there is no solace in the findings of our research, there is at least some consolation in the research itself. . . . The effort to understand the universe is one of the very few things that lifts human life above the level of farce, and gives it some of the grace of tragedy.

But whence arises the law that says that the universe is supposed to have a point, or that if it does, that human consciousness is large enough to understand it? As is any great work of art, the universe is a koan, a riddle whose "answer" lies in living it out. To seek an *answer* to the greatest questions is death to the questions and very probably the questioners. One seeks not to *answer* but to *address*. One commits oneself not to answers but to the lifelong process of searching for the right questions. One opts for reverence over irony.

Ithaka

C. P. Cavafy, trans. Edmund Keeley and Philip Sherrard

As you set out for Ithaka
hope the voyage is a long one,
full of adventure, full of discovery.
. . . .
Keep Ithaka always in your mind.
Arriving there is what you are destined for.
But do not hurry the journey at all.
Better if it lasts for years,
so you are old by the time you reach the island,
wealthy with all you have gained on the way,
not expecting Ithaka to make you rich.

Ithaka gave you the marvelous journey.
Without her you would not have set out.
She has nothing left to give you now.

And if you find her poor, Ithaka won't have fooled you.
Wise as you will have become, so full of experience,
you will have understood by then what these Ithakas mean.

In the same vein, British novelist Jeanette Winterson writes in *Weight*:

That's why I write fiction—so that I can keep telling the story. I return to the problems I can't solve, not because I'm an idiot, but because the real problems

can't be solved. The universe is expanding. The more
we see, the more we discover there is to see. . . . Science
is a story. History is a story. These are stories we tell
ourselves to make ourselves come true.

Seyyed Hossein Nasr, a Muslim historian of science, writes, "Is-
lamic thinkers acquainted with modern science have usually been
aware that the rejection of all purpose in the cosmos by many
scientists is not a scientific statement, but a statement of faith in a
particular ideology." As a skeptic, I have a healthy skepticism of
people who propose to search for and provide answers instead of
celebrating the ongoing search.

Late in Tom Stoppard's brilliant play *Arcadia*, Hannah, the
play's female academic, says to the statistician Valentine and the
humanist Bernard:

It's all trivial. Your grouse, my hermit, Bernard's Byron.
Comparing what we're looking for misses the point. It's
wanting to know that makes us matter.

Which is a much more affirmative and affirming restatement
of Steven Weinberg's point regarding the pointlessness of the universe. Beauty resides not in the outcome but in the search.

*

We are at an all-hands-on-deck moment of history, in which we
must figure out how to learn how to work together or we will surely perish separately. Science, art, religion—we are all facing the
dismantling of the great experiment launched by (among others)
Thomas Aquinas to learn more about ourselves and our world.
All around us we face the rise of fundamentalism, which seeks to
return us to some imagined halcyon prelapsarian state where we
dwell in holy ignorance. Let us be clear on this point: fundamentalism is as great a threat to thoughtful theology and thoughtful art
as it is to thoughtful science.

And so I come back to the question of the nature of progress. Finally I have thrown my lot in with Christianity because I am a Westerner at heart. I have faith that we can nudge the great ship of humanity in a direction of our choosing, and that this direction may favor life over death. I believe in Chekhov's "unceasing movement toward perfection." I believe in George Eliot's "growing good of the world." Following Dr. Martin Luther King, Jr., I believe in the moral arc of the universe inclining toward justice— if only because the alternative is despair, and there is no future in despair.

All around us are promising signs. Among biologists, we see the growing understanding that "survival of the fittest," a phrase coined not by Darwin but by the crackpot eugenicist Herbert Spencer, is not a comprehensive understanding of the world, and that cooperation is as or more important than competition in assuring the survival of species. For the first time in history, we understand the impact of our choices on the planet. Legislators can use that understanding to reward behaviors that make us better citizens and to marginalize behaviors that benefit the individual at the expense of the commonwealth. We can use science as a means to the end of teaching ethics. We can integrate religion— the realm of the sacred—with philosophy, the world of ethics. Artist and scientist, priest and skeptic, we can recognize ourselves in common cause as those who seek Beauty in life.

Do I believe this is going to happen? No, I do not. Only the most determined optimist could ignore the implications of the combination of scientific and historical knowledge. I am not an optimist, though all the same I sustain hope. I read; I write; I work with young people. Six impossible things before breakfast.

Dreamers and Fools:
Notes from Burning Man
(2012)

To a consciousness formed in gentle deciduous lands, the vista is unimaginably bleak: The toxic, colorless void of a Nevada alkali lakebed, a blank white canvas the size of Rhode Island, flat as water and dry as parchment on which there lives nothing visible to the naked eye, remnant of the Pleistocene stretching to a barely visible horizon of tawn and purple mountains. Hot winds blow from all points of the compass and shift direction in an instant, whipping the lakebed into dust devils that spiral into a cloudless blue sky, on occasion building near-tornadic power. At times a steady wind blows for interminable hours, during which alkali dust fine as talc clogs the pores and lungs and reduces the world beyond arm's length to a white blur. We might be inhabitants of one of Calvino's invisible cities except that only mad dogs and white men would attempt to inhabit this godforsaken place. At this moment of the American Empire's decline, this science fiction setting is home for our premier arts festival, anointed by the *Los Angeles Times* as the "current hot ticket" for academic study—the landscape of Burning Man.

Each year, for several weeks artists and pretenders from around the world camp here on the *playa* (Spanish for "beach"), 150 miles north of Reno, laying out streets, building a structure to house basic services (information, medical assistance, security), constructing more and less monumental sculptures and installations, bars, restaurants, dance halls, and New Age amusements—e.g., an outdoor roller-skating disco, or a giant vagina through which you wiggle to be reborn into friends' waiting hands. The playa is the playground of our most powerful image makers—the software engineers and computer graphic designers of Lucasfilm, Pixar, DreamWorks, Google—who flee the constraints of civilization to play in what amounts to a free-wheeling, unregulated protectorate of California.

For the eight-day duration of the festival the central shade structure houses sales of ice and coffee; all other monetary exchanges are prohibited. As part of this gift economy, those who come ("Burners") are asked to bring food and drink sufficient to supply ourselves and share with our neighbors, a policy that inspires 24/7 offerings of free pancakes and open-bar cocktail parties. We are also asked to give something of ourselves in a way that expresses our creative spirit while honoring the festival motto "Leave No Trace"—a visitor at any other time of year should never suspect that for eight days each year fifty-thousand-plus people call this dustbowl home.

Burning Man could have been conceived in San Francisco in part because only fog-bound San Franciscans arrive at summer's end so starved of sun and warmth that even the dusty dried lakebeds of Nevada look attractive; and then there is the city's obsession with drugs and casual sex, both amply in evidence. Hunter Thompson would make easy hay here on the playa, satirizing the naked visitor who calls herself Salmonella, or the hapless husband whose wife has left him, taking their six-month-old child, and who asks my camp to send a collective shout-out via his video camera telling her that we love her, or the personable matron who asks us to test drive the knockout pot brownies baked by her son, or the debates about which drugs are best suited for the evening.

But San Francisco has a history of incubating movements that, for better and worse, went on to influence national and international culture—the Beat Generation and the unrestrained hippies who succeeded it, the Summer of Love and the unrestrained materialism that succeeded it, Silicon Valley and the unrestrained materialism that accompanies it, and now the obsession with sustainability as the politically correct response to the destruction wrought by all that unrestrained materialism.

If we believe what scientists tell us about our future the only intellectually respectable option is despair. Whereas, according to its website, Burning Man offers "part of a solution to our modern malaise." I'm ready to grasp at straws on the premise that they may be attached to floating casinos aboard which my species may gamble with the gods to salvage a future in which I can imagine our children living, and so I go to Burning Man, to discover how it motivates people alienated from church and cynical about government; to find if it may unlock one door to learning and teaching how we may better live in harmony with each other and the planet; to see if it lives up to its hype.

*

Late August 2010: I buy my ticket—three hundred bucks, give or take a few, and meet up with friends to drive hundreds of miles from somewhere to nowhere, arriving at sunset to join a miles-long queue of RVs and rental trucks idling amid the Nevada sagebrush. Hours later we are admitted, and join the homesteaders in staking our claim on the "streets," concentric arcs in the dust some five miles in diameter and having as their focal point a seventy-foot tower constructed of flammable materials and topped by a stylized man.

Encountered in this setting, every created object or spectacle is so improbable as to suggest divine intervention. An undulating metal sound sculpture whose speakers range from tiny to huge, under and around and through which one may wander; a forty-foot-tall globe that spits methane-fueled flames; a multistoried anthill large enough to accommodate tens of people wandering through its mazes; a fifty-foot-tall wire-mesh woman in a pose

drawn from Asian dance and lit from within at night; a grace-
ful shade structure, rebar trees draped with perforated rubbery
scarves, housing a speaker's corner under which a physicist holds
forth on the hoaxes he claims Deepak Chopra perpetrates in the
name of string theory. Among these sculptures roam art cars—
mobile sculptures constructed over a car or a truck or a Hum-
mer. Most marvelously, a life-size silver *Tyrannosaurus rex* opens its
jaws, turns its head, opens and closes great claws and spouts a
roar of flame. The animal kingdom is popular, maybe in homage
to how fast we're depleting it—there are mobile, larger-than-life
barracudas, praying mantises, butterflies, caterpillars. The largest sculptures are in the central playa, but smaller sculptures and
installations are scattered throughout the vast impermanent en-
campment, self-styled Black Rock City. Some (e.g., an ingenious
movie theater, which I access by crawling through a tunnel) are on
the farthest reaches of the perimeter, a beacon and reward for the
drugged or lost who stumble so far from the Man.

Most of the installations are designed to amaze and stupefy,
which isn't much of a challenge when half the audience is on Ecstasy. Boys like to build things up and tear them down, boys like to
blow things up, there will always be boys, witness our endless wars,
watch *Avatar*. If their fiery sculptures leave a lasting impression it
is of awe; and awe, as Edmund Burke pointed out centuries ago,
has its roots in fear—fear of what we can do and of our willingness
to do it.

Love cannot live in the presence of fear. Yet there is—as there
must be—the eternal hope of repair and renewal.

*

Sometime after midnight on the playa: I have been to the Temple of Flux to inscribe the names of the honored dead. Thousands
of people are biking or walking from one installation or camp to
the next, but we might be galaxies in space, so vast are the distances
between us. Then the wind picks up and dust swallows the neon-
lit Man, who becomes a smudge of green light in the darkness.

Glow lamps and headlights that had been wandering haphazardly turn as one as, in obedience to some atavistic instinct, several thousand people seek shelter—no, not shelter, there is no shelter, but only companionship— *communion*—at the feet of the Man.

*

From the Burning Man website, ca. 2011:

> Burning Man is not confined to the artificial limits of Black Rock City. It is more than an event. It has become a social movement. Very typically, participants found significant new relationships or resolve to undertake ambitious projects as a result of their experience. Just as often, they end old relationships, deciding to get divorced or quit their jobs. The typical statement one hears sounds like a conversion experience: "Burning Man has changed my life," and this is manifestly true. Few remain indifferent or return sated.

A fellow Burner tells me she's following the Diamond Heart path, which draws on "every" religious tradition. "Every?" I ask, and in response she lists Buddhism, Sufism, Hinduism, transpersonal psychology, "the somatic connection between the body and the energy fields."

The great three-cornered stool of Western civilization—Judaism, Christianity, and Islam—does not make her list, even as Burning Man's organizers sit firmly astride that stool. The Man-to-be-burned invites comparison to other, more famous martyrs, but more significant is the founders' pervasive belief in redemption, enormous changes at the last minute ("Burning Man has changed my life"), American exceptionalism, *progress*, our most important product. A crooked but unbroken line extends from the "city upon a hill" of John Winthrop's 1630 sermon to his fellow Puritans aboard the *Arabella* to this alkali plain in Nevada. Burners are proselytizers, and the light that animates their eyes not unlike that which I encounter in the eyes of the Jehovah's Witnesses who visit my home Saturday mornings.

As easily as "a solution to our modern malaise," I can see Burning Man as the late-stage expression of the driving force that "conquered" the West, the absolute need of white men to impose our will on nature no matter how remote and forbidding. Its gift economy does not eliminate money but requires that we spend it—a lot of it—before we arrive, in contrast to earlier utopian experiments that presumed frugality. I make myself uncomfortable by pointing out that the drugs that fuel the party arrive as the result of untold suffering, and later I make everyone uncomfortable by questioning how an event can describe itself as an experiment in "radical self-reliance" when it requires thousands of gallons of fossil fuels, twelve-volt batteries, generators, and computerized reservations of rental RVs and trucks.

*

Well past one A.M., I visit Thunderdome, a dimly lit geodesic dome from which two harnesses are suspended. A Barbarella-clad dominatrix selects combatants—in this case, dressed as pink rabbits—who are strapped into the harnesses and provided with padded clubs. The harnesses are hung so as to limit the likelihood of serious mayhem, but the flailing is real and the scene is not pretty. Profanity is the dominant idiom. The elegantly dependent clause is nowhere to be heard.

After one bout I leave Thunderdome to wander far out beyond the noise and crowds and lights and there, in the star-spangled blackness of a moonless Nevada night, stumble on this apparition: a flawlessly recreated 1950s diner, complete with dispensers of flimsy napkins and those stainless steel creamers that spill with every pour. Forty miles from permanent habitation, I clamber onto a round chrome stool upholstered in black leatherette, to be served coffee and a perfectly grilled cheese sandwich, Velveeta and American on white toast. Waitresses wearing matching baby-blue uniforms and sporting two-foot-tall blonde beehives are jawing in Brooklyn accents. Later there will be cheesecake. The Milky Way twinkles overhead. A stray dust devil whirls by. A waitress leans across the counter and tucks two postcards featuring an image of the Dust City Diner in my vest pocket. "Send one of dese to your muddah," she says. "And keep duh uddah one, so that tomorrow when you wake up you'll know this wudden a acid trip or a dream."

Except that it *is* a dream, as strange as any acid trip. The events of my waking life usually require years before they penetrate my sleeping world, but in the week following Burning Man I dream of it every night, drifting in and out of sleep, unsure whether I'm encountering hallucinations or memories.

*

Before the festival opens, crews come together to build camps and art. They help each other, feed each other, take care of each other. Then the gates open to the public and the energy begins to corrupt. By week's end the playa is taken over by thrill seekers wanting drugs, wanting sex, wanting—they don't know what they want, they live in desire and it is a powerful and disruptive force, all those good intentions undermined by mere greed for pleasure, dissatisfaction, again and again we choose the apple over Paradise.

This is the story of the Fall, which all the old stories teach, if only we will listen.

But we never listen. We dismiss the old stories as quaint tales even as every day we act them out. The playa is the very theater of their acting out.

*

Sunrise on the playa. Music drifts from all sides, pop and salsa and under and over all the penetrating bass thump of techno, but never the great classics which even the DJs in the disco era played to greet the dawn. Somewhere an art car is playing over and over "I Want to Know What Love Is," and the pop song seems entirely apropos. Burning Man is about desire, QED, but desire for what? Or whom? Desire to live outside time, in the state the great mystics call "perfect prayer"? Desire to live in God?

In writing the question, I realize for the first time which, of chicken and egg, came first: desire preceded God. With its rules of grammar and syntax, human speech must necessarily be the servant of reason, but desire is the opposite of reason, and so we demand, we require a placeholder, a word to label our nameless longing. And so out of our boundless desire we created God.

Let us cross-examine this logic: By definition, infinity is beyond logic—beyond the capacity of reason to describe or encompass. And yet all the old stories in all the great traditions agree that God is infinite. How then may we know the Unknowable, the Infinite, God, the gods and goddesses? Surely only through that aspect of the human condition that is itself limitless: through our desire, which is not at all the same as sex. The better word is "longing."

Thus through the infinitude of our desire—our longing—may we understand the infinitude of God.

Sometimes I think that God *is* desire, that desire *is* God.

This idea, which strikes our cynical, jaded, prudish twenty-first-century ears as bizarre, was commonplace in the Middle Ages and lay close to the heart of the teachings of some of its most famous preachers and mystics—Bernard of Clairvaux, Abélard, John of the Cross, Teresa of Ávila, Meister Eckhart, Julian of Norwich. Some theologians of the time understood angels as pure desire, an idea that sadly has fallen by the wayside, along with the companion understanding that in the hierarchy of being, angels are inferior to humans, since they are given heaven, whereas we have to earn it.

Every human gesture begins in desire. Our post-Victorian, essentially Protestant culture insists on interpreting "desire" as "sexual desire," when, at least for *Homo sapiens*, the biological itch is merely its literal manifestation, a correlative of a much greater desire—for union, for communion with what many would label God and some would wisely decline to label at all.

In the end the Burning Man experience is so individual as to defy generalization—I write less about what it *was* than what I *wanted it to be.* It sets out to create a sacred space, which calls forth not doctrine and dogma but the dreams that live in our hearts. In a sacred space we live, not in "reality" but in desire—if one must supply a name, in God.

And yet, though Burning Man's concept and execution are religious to their cores, "God" is the word least likely to be heard.

I am perforce aware of the resistance evoked by that Name, of the horrors perpetrated in its service, the abuses that have been heaped on it, the cliché it has become. As a younger, angrier man I rejected it—why name the unnameable? In midlife, possessed of experience and memory, I encounter the answer: Humans, the creatures who tell stories, do not remember or even perceive that which has no name. To name the gods is to seize fire from their hands and, equally important, to assume responsibility for its use. To reject the Name was once my greatest act of courage, but these days I find a greater courage in reclaiming the word—one of the infinite names for what the Burning Man organizers call that aspect of a "natural world exceeding human powers."

A passage comes to mind from a letter of a Trappist monk, a friend of my family:

> The return to God must come, but hard shall He have to strike before people will accept the just and easy solution. . . . The real revolution must be a personal one. Each individual must make it himself.

If Burning Man is fifty thousand nomads in search of a personal revolution, where better to seek it than the desert, archetypal landscape of seekers?

We live in a faithless age, when what so many smart people lack is not belief—there's too much of that, whether belief in the great gray-bearded Guy in the Sky to solve all our problems or belief in the power of technology to solve all our problems. We lack the faith required to live rooted in humility before the unknowable mystery in which we live.

"Citizens of modernity, consumers of violence as spectacle, adepts of proximity without risk, are schooled to be cynical about the possibility of sincerity," wrote Susan Sontag, who as a New Yorker knew whereof she wrote. "Some people will do anything to keep themselves from being moved. How much easier, from one's chair, far from danger, to claim the position of superiority."

Whatever one may write or say of the Burners, they, or at least their organizers, are not in their chairs. If, at a time of declining natural resources, peaceful change is possible, it will manifest itself not, judging from their dismal outcomes, through global climate conferences, but through a new generation teaching themselves (they are not learning this from their elders) the many ways through which less is or can be more. Is it possible, is it imaginable that Burning Man could be one means to that end?

*

Burning Man's organizers understand the power of ideas, so much stronger than armies. And what is their primary motivating idea? That action trumps thought. The last and thus most privileged of Burning Man's guiding principles reads, "Immediate experience is . . . the most important touchstone of value in our culture."

It is an ancient delusion, rooted more in wishful thinking than in fact, that enlightenment resides in unmediated experience. A creature that does not labor to learn and sustain the discipline of paying attention is soon a dead creature. This fact applies to human beings, however our technology—from the pointed stick used to plant the first seed to the so-called smart phone—enables and encourages us to live oblivious to the facts of life, including most particularly death. Thus does Burning Man subscribe to and extend the era of flash and dazzle over pause and think.

All the same, the last of the ten principles continues, "We seek to overcome barriers that stand between us and . . . a natural world exceeding human powers," a phrase that the Burning Man website invokes elsewhere and that reveals a humility not often encountered in the rhetoric of left-wingers or libertarians. What are the implications of this humility? My post–Burning Man dreams feature not flaming globes and Thunderdome but the Dust City Diner and a slow waltz at two A.M. with an old friend wearing a cutaway. The flaming globe and Thunderdome exemplify artists beating their chests; the Dust City Diner and the starlight dance exemplify reaching out. It's the difference between art as narcissism and art as an expression of love.

And art that springs from love just might be one version of William James's "moral equivalent of war," an outlet for all that testosterone that otherwise expresses itself in battle. Love that roots itself in desire—not for combat but for communion, in which a grilled Velveeta sandwich can serve as an entirely adequate Eucharist—an incarnation of humility at our place in "the natural world exceeding human powers."

*

It is a strange and unsettling thing, to watch people choosing to reinvent the wheel. Milling around at the foot of the Man as he's about to be burned, surrounded by fifty thousand drunk, high, screaming people I suppress the urge to shout, "Crucify him! Crucify him!" Most of my fellow Burners wouldn't get the reference and those who did wouldn't like it.

The old myths are sufficient—the patterns are archetypal, repeating not because we want to recycle our costumes (which, strictly speaking, the ritual of renewal forbids) but because time describes not a line but a circle or, more aptly, a spiral, turning back on itself. "Nothing is ever escaped"—James Baldwin. "It all comes back"—Joan Didion. The Christmas crèche must always have its holy infant, its ox and lamb, the hovering angels and the three Magi. Durga may arrive in many colors but she must always have ten arms brandishing ten weapons, must always have her children at her side, must always be crushing beneath her feet the evil blue demon Mahishasura, who must always appear in the form of a water buffalo. The Yaquis of southern Arizona must strip their elaborate masks and pile them on the flames, while they crawl in supplication to the deer dancer. The Man may look different every year but every year he must be put to the torch.

And so we arrive at the timeless, essentially religious questions at the heart of our "modern malaise" that Burning Man organizers seek to resolve: Must we endlessly repeat our old triumphs and mistakes in different guises and settings? Or may we learn from them and progress? But then how do we define progress? Ever fancier gewgaws and gadgets (at least the boys are building art instead of building bombs)? Or a deeper understanding and practice of myth and ritual (the Dust City Diner)? Is history linear or circular? Is Burning Man another means of extending the adolescence of empire, where people denied the triumphs of conquest and exploitation of new continents resort to the Nevada desert to play out fantasies of those triumphs? Or is it a good-faith effort in sagebrush country—heartland of white man's exploitation—to subvert and transform the culture of empire through "leave no trace"?

*

A year and more has passed since I attended Burning Man, but a visit to the website suggests not much has changed. A "sister nonprofit," the Black Rock Arts Foundation, is making small grants to worldwide projects that in many ways meet the festival's ideals more closely than the festival itself, e.g., a Guatemalan school built from recycled plastic bottles. Burning Man uses its website to mobilize volunteers in response to various natural and man-made disasters. It has undertaken to revitalize a "depressed San Francisco neighborhood" without displacing its long-term low-income residents—or so the organizers claim, though the site is vague on how, in the city's crazed real estate market, this is to be accomplished.

Among the fifty thousand attending, the artists and writers seem best prepared to do the slog labor required to turn the wheel of the teachings. But Burning Man presents no apparent challenges to transnational corporate rule or wars of aggression aimed at maintaining the economic power of a declining empire. In fact, the festival is remarkably apolitical, perhaps because many of its principals derive their prosperity from corporate institutions at the heart of our empire (Lucasfilm, DreamWorks, Google, Pixar).

Often I found myself wondering if the organizers could take the bold step of declaring "Burning Green" as an ongoing theme, permanently banning diesel generator-powered installations and limiting RVs to one per camp. What would happen if the festival made such an emphatic statement about our need to wean ourselves from fossil fuel-powered spectacle? *That* would be the ultimate gesture of faith in the festival's capacity to transform and adapt the culture of empire.

Until the organizers make such a dramatic gesture, I have a hard time taking their aspirations seriously, even as I have faith that simply declaring those aspirations gives the next generation a goal. In this sense Burning Man could be read as a paradigm for the whole of our energy-hogging society: Anybody can talk the sustainability talk. But can we walk the sustainability walk?

*

To know the beauty of the kiss the young gymnasts share on their trapeze swings, you must in that same moment know the toxic grit of the ancient lakebed under your nails and chafing your crotch, from days of living in the dust you must know thirst that no water can slake, you must be one with the dust, remember, man, that you are dust and unto dust you shall return. You must know the drive up the granite incline of the Sierras over the pass whose snows took the lives of so many, past the glitter and tack of Reno, through the emptiness of a hundred miles of sagebrush stunted by wind and drought. You must know the drive and all that has come before the drive, your particular dead and the particular ways in which they become present to you in this blank glaring white canvas of dust. You must have held the hand of the dying, you must in the greatness of your grief have kissed their cooling lips. You must know love; you must know loss of love, no, never lost, nothing is ever lost, but the illusion of loss is stronger than the power of presence, you must seek to know presence. You must see the tawdry decadent excess for what it is, bread and circuses, and in that same moment see through it to what lies beyond, the desire to know and be one with each other in union with what we once had the courage to name, what we once called God.

You must know all this and much more at the moment when, standing in white hot pants and scarlet suspenders and a black top hat, you watch a young woman with arms larger than your calves enfold herself in a scarlet drape and, using it as her rope, roll herself many feet skyward to flip and turn in the golden evening light. Across the dust-deviled road the drugged and drunk dance to a rhythmic pounding that mimics and matches the thump of the heart on crystal or the give and take of the pelvic thrust at climax. She reaches the top of her drape many feet above the hard-packed dust only to fall effortlessly and deliberately, catching herself inches shy of broken bones, you must know broken bones, you must break, be broken to be made whole, you must know suffering, you must suffer life.

Epilogue

Light in August
(2016)

Dedicated to Joe Begley, independent as a hog on ice

To weave a horse blanket, a Cheyenne woman first chose a person or cause to which she dedicated her labor. Across the coming months she was bound to live by strictures and rules governing all her conduct but most particularly her work. The weaving served both as a discipline and a prayer. Its completion meant the end not only of her labor but also of its spiritual significance: however beautiful, the object she'd woven became simply another material belonging, transient in the way of all material things. The value of her art lay not in the object it produced but in the process of making it.

To make any kind of art, including most particularly writing, is to undertake a small, voluntary engagement with suffering for the sake of a cause greater than our individual selves. After all, the artist or writer could choose to spend her time shopping or watching television. She chooses instead to give some portion of her time to reading or writing or drawing or painting or dancing or making or composing music. She is choosing to devote her resources to trying to make something beautiful, and her effort is her greatest act of beauty. She is choosing to undertake, in however small a way, a hero's journey. She is making a commitment to art as a spiritual practice—to reading and writing as a spiritual practice.

Some years back I was looking for a Bay Area publicist for the paperback edition of my book *Keeping Faith*, in which I had set out to address what it means for someone who thinks of himself as a skeptic to have and keep faith. A good friend recommended a woman who had been a high-end corporate publicist but had left that world to devote herself to publicizing nonprofit causes dedicated to social justice. So I sent her my book and called her up, to have an uncomfortable conversation in which she declined my request because, she said, she was not a person of faith.

She understood the word "faith" as the exclusive property of those who support anti-gay, anti-immigrant propositions and attend megachurches on Sundays. I tried to convince her that she was the very audience for the book—that the book described my journey toward reclaiming the word "faith." I noted how in undertaking personal sacrifice for worthy causes with no guarantees of success, she was living out the very definition of faith. I pointed out that she was allowing her opponents to define the word for her, rather than taking responsibility to define it for herself. She would have none of it.

On my first day in high school debate club I learned that the side that defines the terms usually wins the debate. Salvation, resurrection, incarnation, blessing, vow, sin, saint, grace, holy, prayer, sacred, joy, even faith, even hope, even love—think about this unhappy fact: how so many of us who love each other and the planet have allowed these words to be taken from us and redefined by the forces of exclusion, fundamentalism, anger, fear.

*

These days we use the words "fact" and "truth" interchangeably, when in *fact*, "fact" is from the same Latin root as the French verb *faire*, "to make." A fact is something made by human hands—look to our verb "manu*fact*ure." Truth, on the other hand, originates with the same word as "troth," a gesture born of good faith. Thus at its heart our very concept of "truth" requires a leap into the unknown—a leap of faith.

Early mystics and prophets did not have access to the vast array of knowledge about our universe that empiricism has given us. But they understood knowledge as in service to truth, rather than the other way around.

I visualize approaches to finding meaning as concentric circles. Empiricism—that is, the belief that knowledge can and will explain the universe—is a seductive and rewarding way of seeing and being, and it occupies one circle. Mysticism constitutes a larger circle that embraces and celebrates knowledge while also embracing ways of knowing that cannot be calibrated or weighed or measured. As sociologist Parker Palmer wrote,

> Why assume that sensation and rationality are the only points of correspondence between the human self and the world? Why assume so, when the human self is rich with other capacities—intuition, empathy, emotion, faith, to name only a few? . . . Does the multiplicity of our modes of knowing suggest a similar multiplicity in the nature of what we know?

We are seeking to know ourselves through facts, when the only way I've come to a greater understanding of myself is through truth. I recall the words of Ghosananda, a Cambodian Buddhist monk and survivor of a concentration camp under Pol Pot, who told me in an interview, "To know suffering is to understand the dharma"— to know, really to *know* suffering is to understand the foundation of what it means to be alive. His observation is not a *fact* but a *truth*.

*

A professor is by definition one who professes. My faith, born of what experience has taught me, is in you, my reader, or more precisely, in the capacity of reading and writing, diligently and mindfully pursued, to open us to a greater understanding of ourselves and of others. From understanding grows compassion; from compassion grows real, enduring, life-affirming change.

Since before Homer we have supported and praised those women and (mostly) men who explored the exterior world. Now, however, Whitman, our national seer and prophet, bears reinvocation: the "circle [is] almost circled" he tells us, and we face home again, very joyous—home being Asia, source of the philosophies that inspired Whitman's *Leaves of Grass* and Emerson's essays and Thoreau's *Walden*. But Whitman concludes "Facing West" with the poignant questions, "But where is what I started for so long ago? And why is it yet unfound?"

The time has arrived for us to undertake the more difficult journey, the journey of self-knowledge, the journey into our interior selves, the voyage of and into the heart. Only he who descends to the underworld can save the beloved. Only she who undertakes the interior journey can save herself. "Explore thyself," Thoreau wrote. "Herein are demanded the eye and the nerve." Thus he sets the prize before us, the city on the distant hill.

Because I believe fervently in the power and necessity of reason, I believe in progress, and here is how my reading and writing have revealed it to me: Working in the thirteenth century from translations of Aristotle obtained from the Arabs, St. Thomas Aquinas, perhaps the greatest voice of reason in Western Europe since classical Rome, posited a pyramid of life with man at its apex, closest to God by virtue of our gift of reason. Charles Darwin began dismantling that pyramid, using reason to show how we are a product of and subject to the same forces that produce the redwood tree and the newt. Lynn Margulis, a biologist and not coincidentally a woman, put forth in the twentieth century the Gaia hypothesis, describing the universe as one great organism in which everything and every creature is interdependent, including humankind. I understand progress as the trajectory of those ideas, each built on its predecessor, and for that reason, despite my deep-seated misgivings and native pessimism, I am guardedly hopeful—not optimistic, but hopeful—about our future.

Science and technology are not the answer for the simple reason that they are not the problem. *We* are the problem. If we are to find our way out of this mess that we have made it must be not only through science and technology, though they will play a necessary role, but by learning to live in harmony with each other and with our fellow creatures. That will require, first and foremost, living in harmony with ourselves. And these are not material but spiritual, or, if you prefer, philosophical, undertakings.

*

To be "everywhere home" is to be nowhere home—such was my first thought on reading Jane Hirshfield's poem that provided the epigraph to this book. I was reacting from deep within the traditions of the West—Europe and its philosophical children. *The Rule of Benedict*, the sixth century book of counsel and regulation that sets down the structure and principles governing most Christian monasteries, emphatically makes the point:

> The fourth kind of monks are those called gyrovagues.
> These spend their lives tramping from province to province,
> staying as guests in different monasteries
> for three or four days at a time.
> Always on the move, with no stability,
> they indulge their own wills
> and succumb to the allurements of gluttony,
> . . . .
> Of the miserable conduct of all such
> it is better to be silent than to speak.

But I have lived many years on the Asia-facing shores of North America, in the course of which I have absorbed, through study and osmosis, a different way of understanding and being in the world. Japanese Zen names this practice *unsui*, "wandering cloud," or *sennin*, "a hermit who lives on dews"—monks who make a home from their journeys, whose practice is to live lightly on the land.

Some years ago Czech playwright and president Václav Havel wrote, "Without a global revolution in human consciousness, nothing will change for the better, and the catastrophe toward which the world is headed . . . will be unavoidable." Consider for a moment how differently we would treat the planet if we perceived and practiced home everywhere—the canyons of the Colorado as well as the lawns of suburban New Jersey, the Mediterranean coast and the West Virginia strip mine, the Big Island and the Superfund site.

No duality, we are all one in Atman, in the Dao, in God, in Beauty, in Christ Jesus, to name a rough chronology in which these principles were articulated. We must teach ourselves anew to think in story, in metaphor, understanding that the best way to illuminate a challenge is often not to approach it head on but through a story or a poem that incarnates the mystery, that gives the mystery flesh and blood and brings it to life for the reader or listener to contemplate.

> Eternity is not a long, long time. Eternity is the opposite of time: It is no time. It is . . . "the now that does not pass away." We cannot reach now by proceeding in mere chronological sequence, yet it is accessible at any moment, as the mysterious fullness of time. . . . We feel at home in that now, in that eternity, because that is the only place where we really *are*. We cannot *be* in the future and we cannot *be* in the past; we can only *be* in the present. We are only real to the extent to which we are living in the present here and now.
> —Brother David Steindl-Rast, OSB

A poem from our national saint and mystic Emily Dickinson makes the same point:

> Forever—is composed of Nows—
> 'Tis not a different time—

*

Every summer, around the beginning of August, a day arrives when I'm walking along in midafternoon and I realize the light has slipped. Its angle is no longer that of high summer, high and hammering—light that for the past couple of months I've come to take for granted, in my too-human fashion, as the way things will always be. Summer will never end. No one I love will ever die.

Now the angling light signals that the endless summer is ending. In fact I and everyone I love will die. The question is only who will be first to reach the finish line.

And yet I see I have indulged a commonplace misperception, since properly understood there is no finish line. We are creatures of light, sentient bundles of energy moving through the universe, it is of us as we are of it, there is no death, there is only process, changing from one form to another. Through some Cartesian sleight of hand the brain refuses to perceive this. Instead it cunningly divides the world into dualities. There's a little dab of brain, I'm told, given over to setting boundaries: this is where I end, this is where you begin—me/you, us/them, male/female, light/dark, beginning/end, life/death.

No doubt these illusions are or were necessary for our survival, no matter that they're the basis for murder and mayhem and our self-centered misunderstanding of death as now-you-see-us, now-you-don't. In fact death is only another milepost in the never-ending becoming of what is. Ask your dog—she'll agree; look to the wag in her tail. You don't see *her* moping about impending doom.

In this particular early August I noticed the slipping light on a walk rendered poignant by the tension of unrequited love. Denied an outlet for my passion, I offered my companion the observation that if I believed in death I'd kill myself. "What do you mean?" he asked, no doubt casting an uneasy glance at the penknife dangling from my knapsack. "All that loss," I answered, "all that grief. Who could stand it, if he really believed death to be the finish line?" Not me. I take great affirmation and good cheer knowing we're light from light, true gods from true gods, one form of energy changing into another until billions of years hence, when in the entropy of time all our colors will merge and melt into a uniformly still gray, the gray of the paintings that hang in the Rothko Chapel in Houston.

Under the auspices of *Harper's Magazine*, I once moderated a debate held in that chapel. The subject at hand was faith and reason, as false a duality as light/dark or male/female or life/death, but one thing had led to another and here we were, with the Pulitzer-winning novelist Marilynne Robinson representing faith and the Nobel-winning physicist Steven Weinberg representing reason and me wondering how I had gotten myself from my childhood in the Knobs into refereeing such august company.

I chose the Rothko Chapel as our venue—a mistake. It features works by Mark Rothko, painted in the decade before he took his life in 1970—vast lozenges of a smooth, even gray surrounded by haloes of an almost indiscernibly darker gray hung against the lighter gray of the walls. Their enveloping gray stillness prompts not debate but contemplation. They demand that we sit down, shut up, still ourselves to the essence of being, the unbearable gray light-ness of being.

Robinson burned with quiet passion. Weinberg might be the most articulate man with whom I have had the honor of conversing, as was evidenced in that day's debate, in which he, the combative atheist, set forth the case for faith, then argued with himself while the contemplative Robinson listened.

But we're not yet at the debate, we've just walked into the chapel and are spending a moment looking at Rothko's paintings. Weinberg shook his head. "I love abstract art," he said. "I collect abstract art. But I just don't get Rothko. What is it with these great blobs of gray." The most delicate of pauses ensued before Robinson said quietly, "It's the moment before creation."

I would have been happy to have ended the debate right there, since to my mind the exchange said all that needed to be said about the debaters' different understandings of the way things are. In *The First Three Minutes* Weinberg wrote, "Even when physicists have gone as far as they can go . . . there seems to be an irreducible mystery that science will not eliminate." Robinson, the contemplative, grasped what he, the scientist, had not perceived: stories and art are our means of putting our hearts around the irreducible mystery. Rothko had painted that mystery a few years before he plunged in.

To reunify the parts of our broken selves is, it seems to me, to make the commitment to become a whole person, a holy person, a vocation that each of us must discern and fulfill in our particular ways. The good news is that, as Rabbi Menachem of Kotzk wrote, there is nothing so whole as a broken heart. Reading and writing are or can be the glue, one means we use to patch ourselves together—they have served that purpose for me.

Among the most brilliant of book titles is William Faulkner's *Light in August*—a novel contained in a phrase. "Memory believes before knowing remembers," Faulkner wrote. "Believes longer than recollects, longer than knowing even wonders." To read or write poetry or prose is to lay claim to your citizenship among the people of faith.

Everything is always, as my friend Barry says, most especially us and most especially memory, and before you ask what he'd been smoking, take a walk at eventide in the light in August, the month of plenitude and of loss.

Note to the Reader

Of the essays collected here, the earliest was published in 1989; the most recent are contemporary and unpublished. Excepting the occasional nip to improve continuity, or tuck to eliminate duplications, I have resisted the impulse to modify or update previously published works—with one exception: "Journals of the Plague Years," which introduces essays written in response to the AIDS epidemic. Each essay transcends, I hope, its historical moment, at the same time providing a snapshot of that moment essential to its meaning and impact. In particular, I have not revised the essays about faith and religion to address the ongoing revelations of sexual abuse by clergy and monastics, a subject I address in my book *Keeping Faith: A Skeptic's Journey among Christian and Buddhist Monks.*

Acknowledgments

It would be impossible to acknowledge all the friends, colleagues, and editors who helped shape this book over almost three decades, but some names come immediately to mind: Shirley Abbott, my lifelong literary confidante; Haney Armstrong; Jane Clayton; Barbara Kingsolver; Sue Luttner; Greg Miller; Barry Owen; and Kathy Seligman. Of my many patient and able editors I thank especially Brian Bouldrey, Susan Brenneman, Eric Copage, Mark Danner, and Amy Rennert. For the earlier essays, Malaga Baldi represented me ably and passionately, placing the first of my essays with the *New York Times Magazine*. Ellen Levine and her assistant Alexa Stark at Trident Media Group are the not-often-enough-acknowledged foundation of my publishing life. Sarah Gorham, editor of Sarabande, was enthusiastic from the first, enabling the sum to become greater than its parts.

My deepest respect and greatest thanks go to the people who entrusted their stories to me—strangers, friends, family.

Publication Acknowledgments

"North of the South, West of the West," published as "California Dreaming," *New York Times Magazine*, May 13, 1990.

"Catholic in the South," *Virginia Quarterly Review*, Summer 1990.

"Father to the Mother," published as "How I Spent My Summer Vacation," *New York Times Magazine*, October 1, 1989.

"Basketball Days," broadcast on National Public Radio's *All Things Considered*, March 29, 1996.

"After Shock in San Francisco," published as "Aftershock in San Franciso," *New York Times Magazine*, June 17, 1990.

"The Limitless Heart," *New York Times Magazine*, June 23, 1991.

"Lucky Fellow," *New York Times Magazine*, May 9, 1993.

"Safe(r) Sex," published as "Safe Sex," *Mother Jones*, September/October 1992.

"City of Innocence and Plague," *Love, Castro Street: Reflections of San Francisco*, edited by Katherine V. Forrest and Jim Van Buskirk, Alyson Books, 2007.

"From the Depths: Oscar Wilde's *De Profundis* in Its Second Century," published as "*De Profundis*," *50 Gay/Lesbian Books Everyone Must Read*, edited by Richard Canning, Alyson Books, 2009.

"Power and Obedience: Restoring Pacifism to American Politics," *Appalachian Heritage*, Winter 2014.

"Ordinary Acts," *The Writer's Journal: 40 Contemporary Writers and Their Journals*, edited by Sheila Bender, Delta, 1997.

"God, Gays, and the Geography of Desire," *Wrestling with the Angel: Faith and Religion in the Lives of Gay Men*, edited by Brian Bouldrey, Riverhead Books, 1995.

"Beyond Belief," published as "Beyond Belief: A Skeptic Searches for an American Faith," *Harper's Magazine*, September 1998.

Some sections of "Shrines and Wonders" first appeared as "Pilgrimage to the Magdalen" in *Terrain: A Journal of Built and Natural Environments*, Spring/Summer 2012, and others were first published as "The Lion and the Lamb" in *Tell Me True: Memoir, History, and Writing a Life*, edited by Patricia Hampl and Elaine Tyler May, published by Borealis Books/Minnesota Historical Society, 2008.

"Dreamers and Fools," published as "Burning Man, Desire, and the Culture of Empire," *Tikkun*, Summer 2012.

"Light in August," *The Louisville Review*, Fall 2014.

About the Author

Fenton Johnson grew up near Kentucky's Trappist monastery, the Abbey of Gethsemani. He has published two memoirs, *Geography of the Heart* and *Keeping Faith: A Skeptic's Journey among Christian and Buddhist Monks*, as well as three award-winning novels: *Scissors, Paper, Rock*; *Crossing the River*; and *The Man Who Loved Birds*. *Geography* won American Library Association and Lambda Literary Awards. He writes regularly for *Harper's Magazine* and teaches in the creative writing programs at the University of Arizona and Spalding University.

Sarabande Books is a nonprofit literary press located in Louisville, KY, and Brooklyn, NY. Founded in 1994 to champion poetry, short fiction, and essay, we are committed to creating lasting editions that honor exceptional writing. For more information, please visit sarabandebooks.org.